SCOTTISH CERTIFICATE OF EDU

General BIOLOGY

The Scottish Certificate of Education Examination Papers
are reprinted by special permission of
THE SCOTTISH QUALIFICATIONS AUTHORITY

ISBN 0 7169 9260 4
© *Robert Gibson & Sons, Glasgow, Ltd., 1998*

ROBERT GIBSON · Publisher
17 Fitzroy Place, Glasgow, G3 7SF.

SCOTTISH
CERTIFICATE OF
EDUCATION

Time – 1 hour 30 minutes

BIOLOGY
STANDARD GRADE
General Level

INSTRUCTIONS TO CANDIDATES

1. All questions should be attempted.

2. The questions may be answered in any order but all answers are to be written in the spaces provided in this answer book, and must be written clearly and legibly in ink.

3. Rough work, if any should be necessary, as well as the fair copy, is to be written in this book. Additional space for answers and for rough work will be found at the end of the book. Rough work should be scored through when the fair copy has been written.

4. Before leaving the examination room this book must be given to the Invigilator. If you do not, you may lose all the marks for this paper.

CONTENTS

1994 Biology — General Level	3
1995 Biology — General Level	25
1996 Biology — General Level	50
1997 Biology — General Level	77
1998 Biology — General Level	105

COPYING PROHIBITED

Note: This publication is **NOT** licensed for copying under the Copyright Licensing Agency's Scheme, to which Robert Gibson & Sons are not party.

All rights reserved. No part of this publication may be reproduced; stored in a retrieval system; or transmitted in any form or by any means — electronic, mechanical, photocopying, or otherwise — without prior permission of the publisher Robert Gibson & Sons, Ltd., 17 Fitzroy Place, Glasgow, G3 7SF.

1. (a) The results in the table below were obtained from a population survey of dandelion plants in a field.
The counts were taken using a quadrat.

Quadrat number	1	2	3	4	5	6	7	8	9	10
Number of dandelions	15	20	12	10	5	2	6	8	12	10

On the grid provided, **complete the bar chart** of the results to show:

(i) the scale and axis;

(ii) the plot for **all** the results.

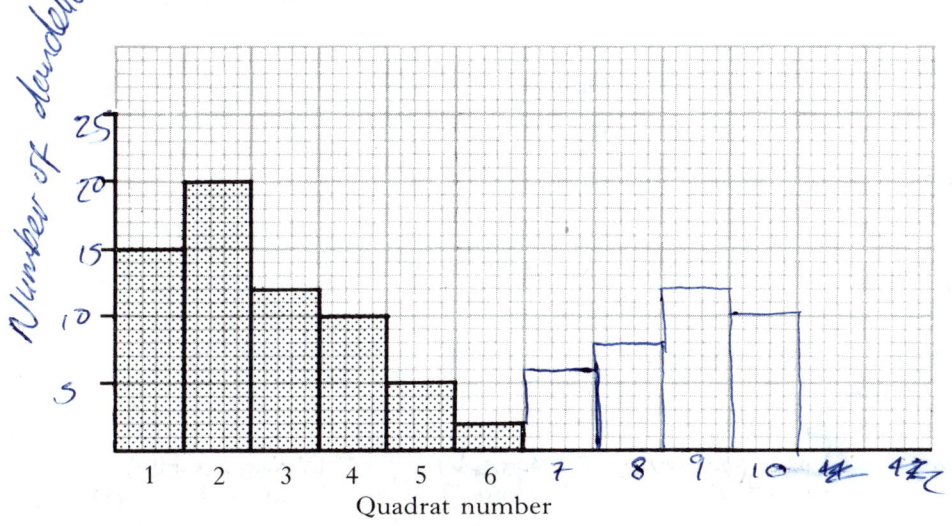

(2)

(iii) Calculate the average number of dandelions in a quadrat.

Space for calculation

Average number ___10___ (1)

(b) This field is part of an ecosystem containing different habitats which support several populations of organisms.

Write the definition of each of the words underlined into the table below.

Word	Definition
Ecosystem	A ~~place where~~ community + habitat
Habitat	a place where an organism lives
Population	a group of organisms of one ~~type~~ type.

(3)

(c) The diagram below shows part of a food web in a freshwater pond.

(i) Use **four** organisms from the food web to construct a food chain in the spaces below.

Duckweed → Mayfly larvae → Dragonfly → Diving beetles
Organism 1 — Organism 2 — Organism 3 — Organism 4 (1)

(ii) The trout and the diving beetles are in competition with each other.

State why they are said to be in competition.

They _____

_____ (1)

(iii) Describe **one** possible **effect** of competition between organisms.

_____
_____ (1)

(iv) State **two** ways by which energy can be lost from a food web.

1. _____heat_____

2. _____waste_____ (2)

(d) Below is a key which can be used to identify some freshwater animals.

KEY

1. Animal with shell   Go to 2
   Animal without shell   Go to 3

2. Shell with two halves hinged together   *Bivalve*
   Shell is a single coil   *Water snail*

3. Body not made up of sections (segments)   Go to 4
   Body made up of segments   Go to 5

4. Tubular body   *Roundworm*
   Flattened body   *Flatworm*

5. Legs absent   *Leech*
   Legs present   Go to 6

6. Three pairs of legs   *Dragonfly nymph*
   Four pairs of legs   *Spider*

(i) **Use the key** to identify the **two** animals shown in the diagrams below.

Name __Dragonfly nymph__   Name __roundworm__ (2)

(ii) **Use the key** to identify **two** features of a leech.

Feature 1. __does not have a shell__

Feature 2. __no legs__ (1)

2. (a) The diagram below shows parts of a flower.

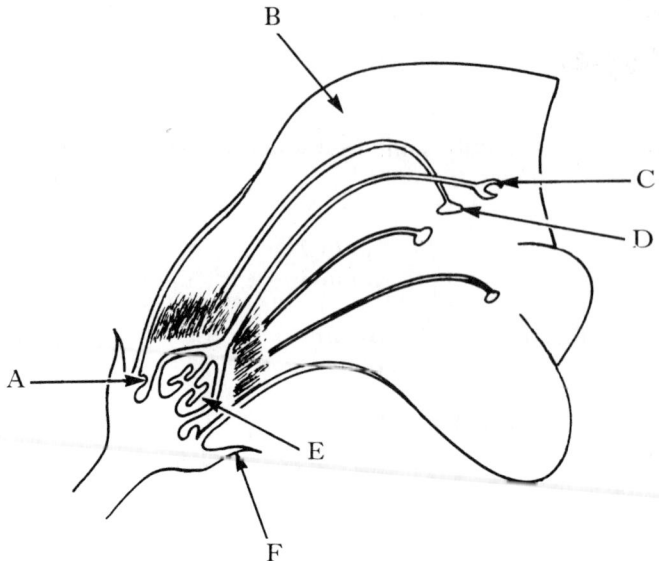

(i) **Use the letters** from the diagram to match the **structures** in Table 1 and to match the **functions** in Table 2.

Table 1

Structure	Letter
Nectary	A
Ovary	E
Stigma	C

Table 2

Function	Letter
Produces pollen	D
Protects the flower when in bud	B

(2+1)

(ii) Name the method of pollination used by this flower.

Method of pollination ___Insect pollination___ (1)

(b) Three twigs from the same plant, with leaves of equal surface area, were set up as shown in the diagrams below.

A   **B**   **C**

Film of oil
100 cm³ water

Upper leaf surfaces covered in vaseline   Lower leaf surfaces covered in vaseline   Neither leaf surfaces covered in vaseline

The experiments were left in identical environmental conditions for 48 hours.

The results in the table below show the volume of water remaining in each cylinder.

Cylinder	Volume of water remaining (cm³)
A	76
B	90
C	65

(i) **Calculate** the **rate of water loss per hour** from the leaves in cylinder A.

Space for calculation

Rate of water loss _____ cm³/hour   **(1)**

(ii) The leaf surfaces contain pores through which water vapour is lost.

Name these pores. Give **one** other function of these pores.

Name _____   **(1)**

Function _____

_____   **(1)**

(iii) Covering the leaf surface with a vaseline coat, blocks the leaf pores.

What conclusion can you come to about the number of pores in the upper and lower leaf surfaces of this plant?

_____

_____ (1)

(iv) Apart from being from the same plant, state **one** other feature of the leaves which **must** be the same so that the comparison of the results is fair.

_____

_____ (1)

(v) If oil was not added to the cylinders, the results obtained would be inaccurate. Why would this be the case?

_____

_____ (1)

3. (a) Diagram A shows some of the structures of the human breathing system.

Diagram B shows a magnification of a small region X of the lung.

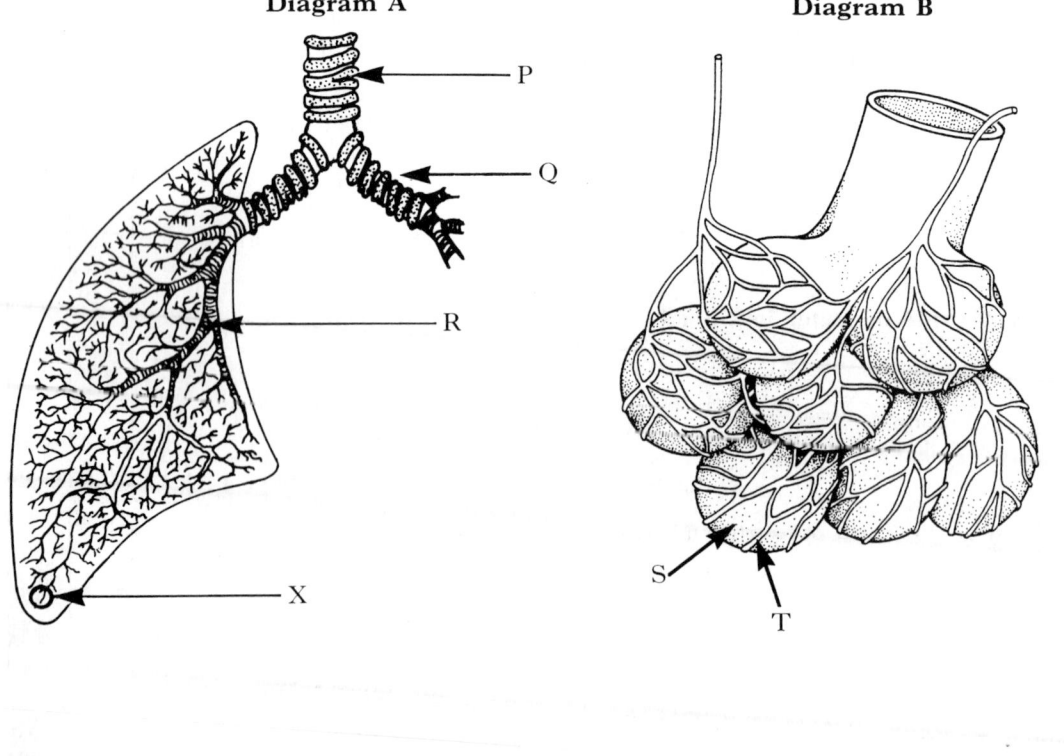

Diagram A **Diagram B**

8

Using letters from the diagrams, complete the table below.

Structure	Letter
Bronchus	l
Capillary blood vessel	
Air sac	J

(2)

(b) Complete the following sentences.

When air is breathed out, it contains more ___Carbon dioxide___ than air breathed in. (1)

The gas which is transported in the red blood cells is ___Oxygen___ (1)

(c) An average adult at rest takes 16 breaths each minute and exchanges 500 cm³ of air with each breath. During exercise, an additional 3000 cm³ of air can be exchanged with each breath and the breathing rate increases to 25 breaths per minute.

Using the information above, answer the following questions.

(I) What evidence is there that there is a change in the breathing rate as a result of exercise?

___Your breathing rates changes from 16 breaths per minute to about 25 breaths.___ (1)

(II) Apart from breathing rate, state one other change which occurs in the pattern of breathing, as a result of exercise.

___Can exinge more air with each breath.___ (1)

(III) Calculate the total volume of air exchanged per minute during exercise.

Space for calculation

_____ cm³ (1)

4. (*a*) The diagram shows the volume of blood flowing to various parts of the body, when at rest and during exercise.

The blood flow is measured in cm³ per minute.

Diagram showing blood flow (cm³/min) to body parts:

At rest: Brain 750, Heart 250, Muscle 1200, Skin 500, Rest of body 3100.

Light exercise: 750, 750, 12400, 1900, (600).

Maximum exercise: 750, 1000, 22000, 600, 650.

Table of total blood flow per minute

	At rest	Light exercise	Maximum exercise
Total blood flow per minute	5800 cm³	17 400 cm³	25000 cm³

(i) **Complete the table** by inserting the value for the total blood flow per minute during maximum exercise.

Space for calculation (1)

750
1000
22000
600
650

(ii) Describe the changes in blood flow to the muscles and to the skin, when going from rest to light exercise and then to maximum exercise.

1. Muscles _it goes up at light exercise and nearly doubles at maximum exercise_ (1)

2. Skin _It goes up by more than half at light exercise and then goes down to nearly it's rest time at maximum exercise._ (1)

(iii) Which part of the body does not experience any change in blood flow, as the result of exercise?

Part of the body _Brain_ (1)

(iv) By how many times does the total blood flow per minute increase, from being at rest to taking light exercise?

Space for calculation

25000
5800
19200

Number of times _____ (1)

(c) The diagram below shows a model of an artificial kidney machine.

As blood passes along the tubing, materials pass into the surrounding fluid from the blood.

(i) What is the purpose of using coiled rather than straight tubing within the kidney machine?

_____

_____ (1)

(ii) Name the waste product which would build up in the body if the kidneys were damaged.

Waste product _____ (1)

5. (*a*) Four test tubes were set up as shown below.

The test tubes were left in a water bath set at 37 °C for 30 minutes.

Urease is an enzyme which breaks down urea to form ammonia.

Any ammonia released is detected by the test papers.

A — Distilled water and urease
B — Urine and urease
C — Plasma from renal artery and urease
D — Plasma from renal vein and urease

The results are shown in the table below.

Test tube	A	B	C	D
Test for ammonia	negative	positive	positive	negative

Use the results to answer the following questions.

(i) Which tubes contained urea?

A + D (1)

(ii) Why were the tubes incubated at 37 °C?

It is the human temperature (1)

(iii) Account for the difference in the **res**ults obtained from the two plasma samples.

(1)

(b) The graph below refers to the activity of two enzymes.

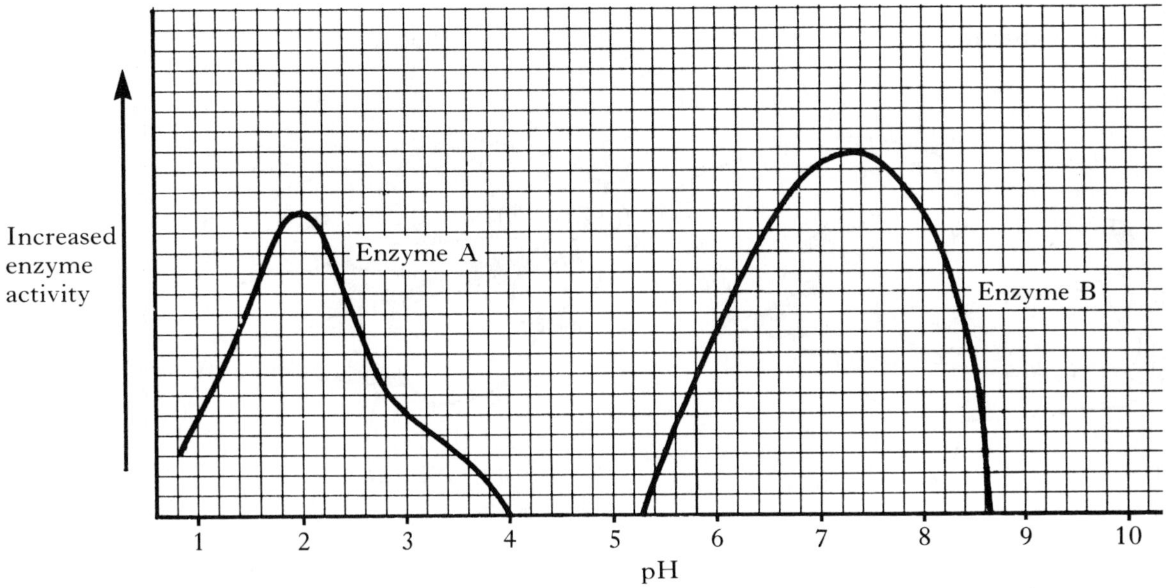

(i) Describe the effects of change in pH on enzyme activity.

_____

_____

_____ (2)

(ii) Which graph would be representative of the action of the enzyme pepsin?

Graph _____ (1)

6. (a) The diagrams below are of the skulls of two different mammals.

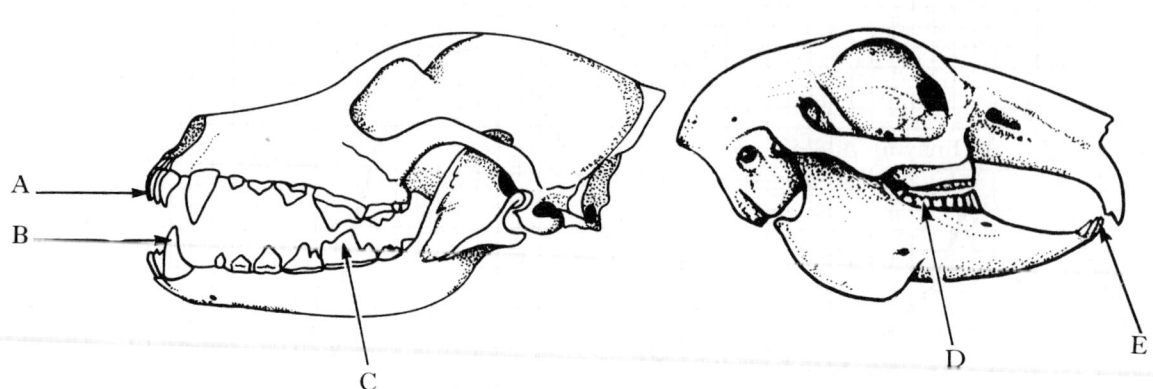

Skull 1 **Skull 2**

Decide if each of the following statements about the diagrams is **TRUE** or **FALSE** and **tick the correct box**.

If the statement is **FALSE, write the correct word in the Correction box** to replace the part of the statement *underlined*.

Statement	True	False	Correction
Tooth B is an *incisor* and is used for piercing flesh	✓		
Skull 2 is that of a *herbivore*	✓		
A type of tooth which is moved in a side-to-side action to shred food is shown by *label C*.		✓	Label D

(3)

(b) The graph shows the changes in mouth pH with time.

If the pH falls below 5·5, the teeth are at risk of decay.

Person A has three meals during the day.

Person B has frequent sugary snacks during the day.

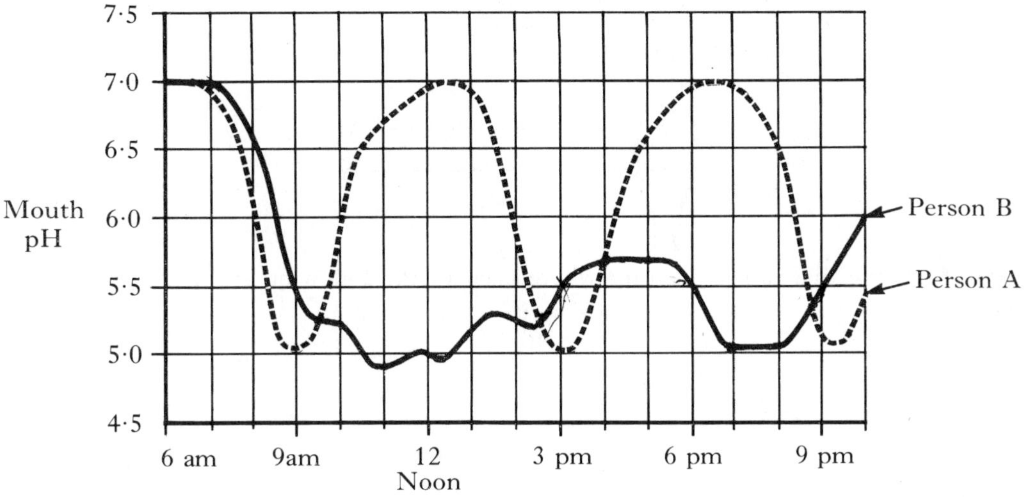

(i) How many times did the mouth pH of person A fall below the level at which there is risk of tooth decay?

Number of times ___3___ (1)

(ii) What is the total length of time person B had levels of mouth pH during which there was a risk of tooth decay?

___9___ hours (1)

(iii) What is the range of mouth pH shown by person A?

___low___ (1)

7. (a) The diagram below shows some of the structures of the human female reproductive system.

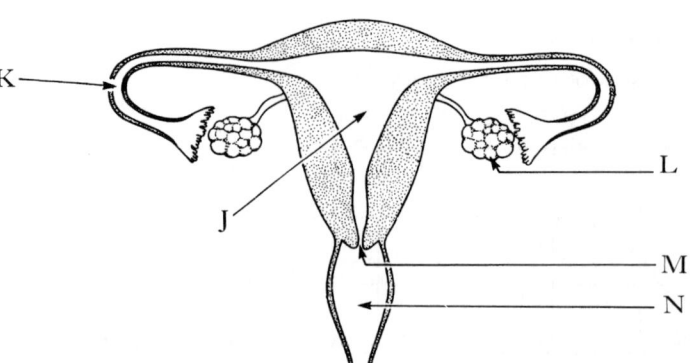

Use a letter from the diagram to identify where each of the following events takes place.

Event	Letter
Production of eggs	
Fertilisation	
Development of embryo	

(2)

(b) The diagram below shows the inheritance of **X** and **Y** chromosome by a human embryo.

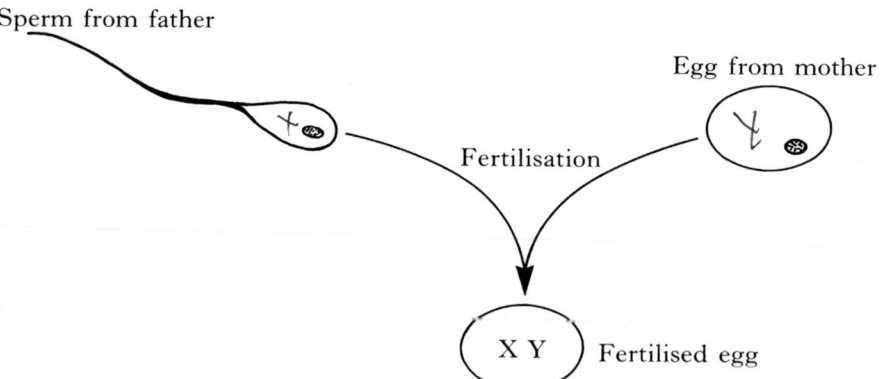

(i) **Complete the diagram** by inserting the appropriate chromosome letter into the egg and the sperm, to show this inheritance. (1)

(ii) The fertilised egg will develop into an individual.

Identify what will be the sex of this individual.

Sex of individual ___male___ (1)

(c) Normal night vision and night blindness (*the inability to see in dim light*) are controlled by two forms of a gene.

The family tree below shows the inheritance of night blindness.

The original parents were both true-breeding.

The key shows the phenotypes of individuals in the family tree.

KEY ☐ Night blind males   ○ Night blind females
         ■ Normal sighted males   ● Normal sighted females

PARENTS: Alan (☐) — Betty (●)

F1: Carol (●) – David (■), Gordon (■), Fiona (●), Jackie (●), Harry (■), Iris (●) – Hamish (☐)

F2: Fred (■), Laura (●), Mandy (●), Norma (○); Dougie (■), Pam (○)

(i) **Use the information** from the F1 generation to identify which form of the gene is dominant (night blind or normal sight).

Give a reason for your answer.

Dominant form ___Normal___ (1)

Reason ___There are more male normal sighted___ (1)

(ii) Other than the original parents, Alan and Betty, identify **two** other people who are true-breeding.

1. ___Dougie___   2. ___Pam___ (1)

(iii) What evidence is there that Carol is **not** true-breeding?

_____

_____ (1)

(d) Both the bar chart and the histogram below refer to a group of 200 people.

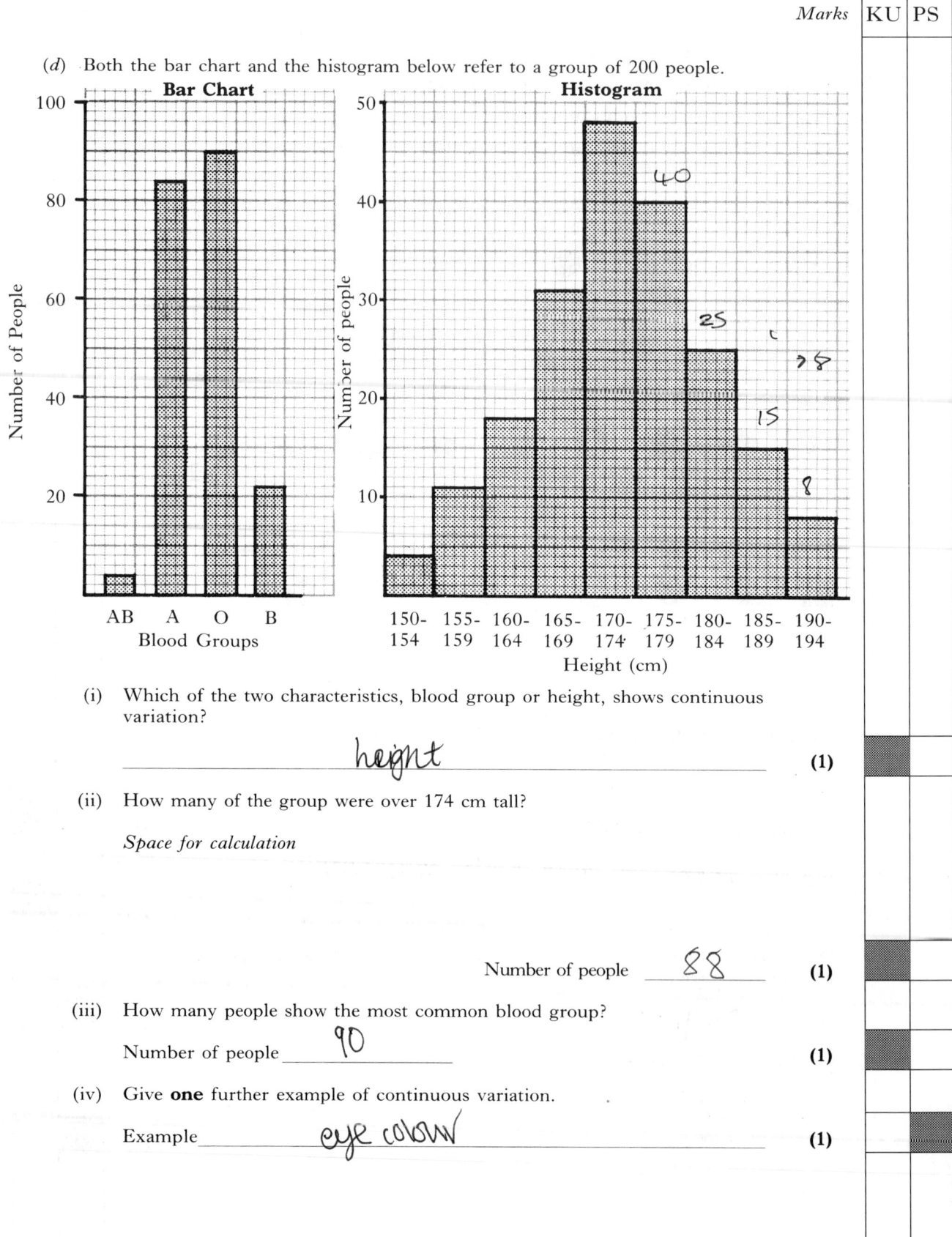

(i) Which of the two characteristics, blood group or height, shows continuous variation?

height (1)

(ii) How many of the group were over 174 cm tall?

Space for calculation

Number of people _88_ (1)

(iii) How many people show the most common blood group?

Number of people _90_ (1)

(iv) Give **one** further example of continuous variation.

Example _eye colour_ (1)

8. (a) The diagram below shows some of the structures in a human eye.

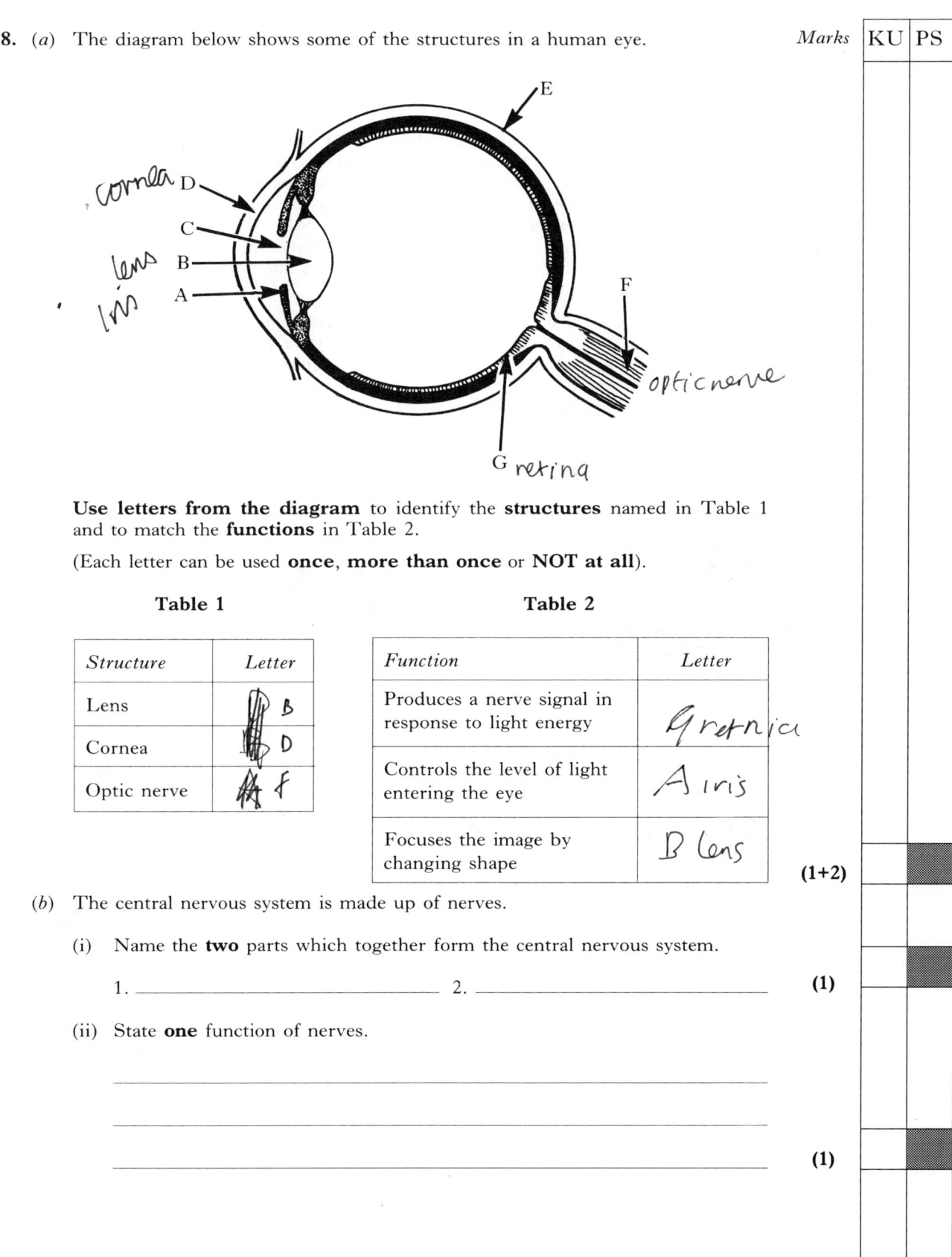

Use letters from the diagram to identify the structures named in Table 1 and to match the functions in Table 2.

(Each letter can be used once, more than once or NOT at all).

Table 1

Structure	Letter
Lens	B
Cornea	D
Optic nerve	F

Table 2

Function	Letter
Produces a nerve signal in response to light energy	G retina
Controls the level of light entering the eye	A iris
Focuses the image by changing shape	B lens

(1+2)

(b) The central nervous system is made up of nerves.

(i) Name the two parts which together form the central nervous system.

1. _____ 2. _____ (1)

(ii) State one function of nerves.

_____

_____

_____ (1)

9. Carefully read the following passage.

Adapted from *Life in a Plant Cell Wall* by Stephen Fry.
(Biological Science Review 4.1)

The living part of every plant cell is neatly packaged within a plant cell wall. The chief chemical substance of a plant cell wall is cellulose. However, plant cell walls are not made up of cellulose alone. Plants have developed cell walls which are complicated. The cell walls of a growing plant are built up from at least six different
5   sugars; at least two structural proteins; about twenty different enzymes and small quantities of many other substances. Cell walls are complex structures and this complexity must be important to plant life. Cell walls, therefore, must not be seen simply as "cardboard boxes".

Cell walls can be removed from plant cells by treating the cells with appropriate
10 digestive enzymes in sugar solution. The resulting cells, now without their walls, can remain alive for several days and are called "protoplasts". They differ from the original cells in several ways, including:
(1)   neighbourliness – they are freely floating independent cells instead of being organised together in tissue;
15 (2)   size – they have no fixed volume. When put into pure water, they swell and burst. Normal plant cells cannot swell beyond a certain size when placed in pure water.

The diagrams below show the structure of a normal leaf cell and a protoplast.

Normal leaf cell

Protoplast

Answer the following questions which relate to the passage.

(*a*) Identify **three** components of a plant cell wall.

1. *cellulose*
2. *sugars*
3. *enzymes*   (1)

(*b*) State the function of the digestive enzymes (line 10).

_____

_____   (1)

(c) The cells swell due to water entering by diffusion (lines 15–17). What term do we use to mean diffusion of water into a cell?

Term used *plasmid* (1)

(d) Why should cell walls not be thought of as "cardboard boxes" (line 8)?

Because they are complex structures + important to plant life. (1)

(e) What is a protoplast (line 11)?

cell (1)

(f) Name **two** cell structures, present in a protoplast, which are also present in animal cells.

1. _____

2. _____ (1)

(g) What is meant by the term *neighbourliness* in the passage (line 13)?

_____

_____

_____ (1)

(h) The passage describes differences between a protoplast and a normal plant cell. Select from the diagrams, **one** other difference between them.

Difference _____

_____ (1)

10. An investigation was carried out into changes in the dry mass of germinating seeds of the same species. Groups of seeds were treated as follows.

   Group A was grown in white light.
   Group B was grown in green light.
   Group C was grown in darkness.

Each day, over a period of 20 days, five germinating seeds from each group were selected at random.

The sample seeds were dried in an oven set at 100 °C to constant mass, in order to obtain their dry mass.

The results are plotted on the graph below.

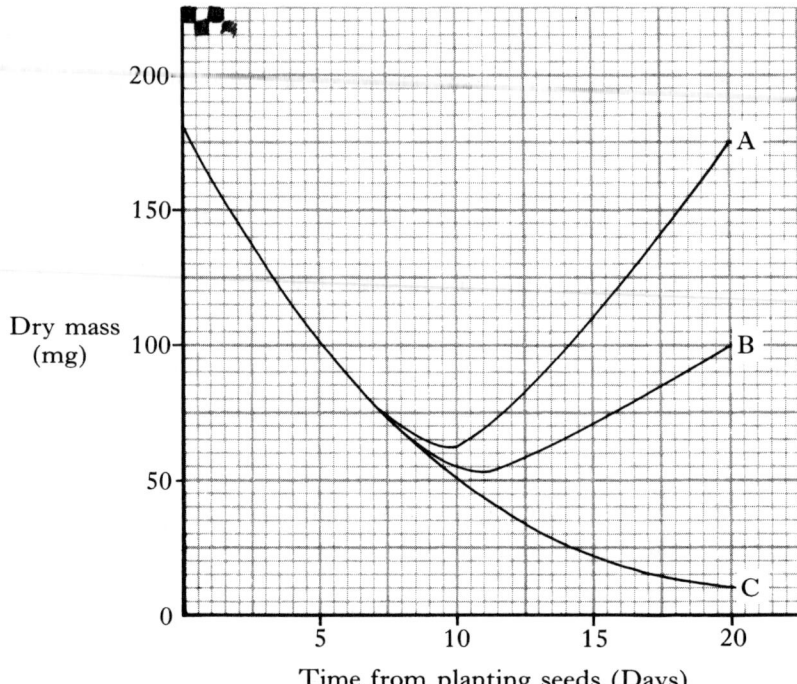

(a) For how many days, during the investigation, does each group decrease in dry mass?

   Group A _____ days

   Group B _____ days

   Group C _____ days   (2)

(b) What is the importance of the seeds being dried to constant mass?

_____

_____   (1)

(c) Why is the validity of the results improved by selecting five germinating seeds to be dried, rather than a single seed?

_____

_____ (1)

(d) Account for the changes in dry mass shown by the samples from Groups A and B during the **last** 10 days of the investigation.

_____

_____

_____ (1)

(e) After how many days did the seeds in Group C show a 50% decrease in dry mass?

After _____ days (1)

(f) Express as a **simple** ratio, the dry mass of Group A seedlings to Group C seedlings, on day 16 of the investigation.

Space for calculation

Ratio _____ Group A: _____ Group C (1)

(g) Name **two** conditions that all seeds need for germination.

1. _____

2. _____ (1)

11. (a) Complete the table below, which refers to two types of movable joint.

Type of joint	Example	Range of movements
	Elbow	
Ball and socket		

(2)

(b) The following diagrams show a model of the human leg in a resting position and in one other position.

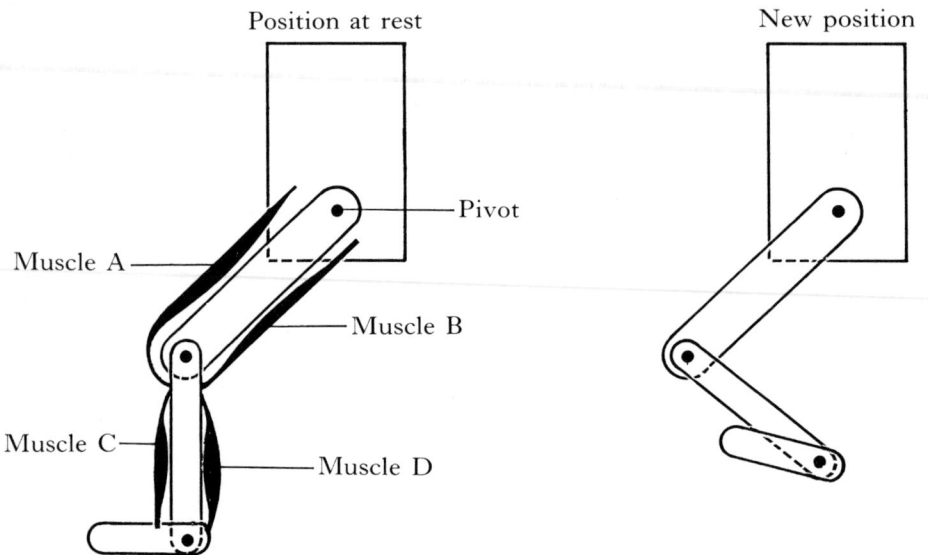

Which **two** muscles contracted to bring about the change from rest to the new position?

Use the letters to identify the muscles.

Muscle _____ and muscle _____ (1)

SCOTTISH CERTIFICATE OF EDUCATION 1995

THURSDAY, 11 MAY
9.30 AM – 11.00 AM

BIOLOGY
STANDARD GRADE
General Level

1. (a) Measurements of soil moisture levels were taken in an area of grass using the meter shown in the diagram below.

Six readings were taken at sites chosen at random on two different days. The results are shown in the table below.

Moisture readings on day 1 (units)	Moisture readings on day 2 (units)
4	7
5	6
4	8
3	6
5	7
4	8

(i) Suggest a reason why the readings on day 2 are all higher than the readings on day 1.

It rained more on day 2. (1)

(ii) Calculate the average of the moisture readings on day 2.

Space for calculation

Average moisture reading ___7___ units (1)

(iii) Explain why six readings were taken each day, rather than one reading.

6 readings were taken instead of one because during the day the dampness of the soil changes and it might also rain during the day. (1)

(b) An area of grass is an example of an ecosystem. In addition to animals and plants, name **one** other part of an ecosystem.

pond (1)

(c) The sentences below give information about organisms found on farmland.

(i) Rabbits on the farm feed on grass and dandelions.

(ii) The rabbits are preyed upon by both stoats and foxes.

Use the information in the sentences to construct a food web in the space below.

[Hand-drawn food web showing grass and dandelions at bottom with arrows up to rabbit, and arrows from rabbit up to stoat and fox]

(2)

(d) Complete the sentence below.

The arrows in a food web show _energy_ flow. (1)

2. (*a*) The average heights of some tree species are given in the table below.

Species of tree	Average height of tree species (m)
Douglas fir	50
Beech	40
Common oak	28
Mountain ash	8
Scots pine	36

(i) On the grid below, complete the bar chart to show the average height of each of the tree species.

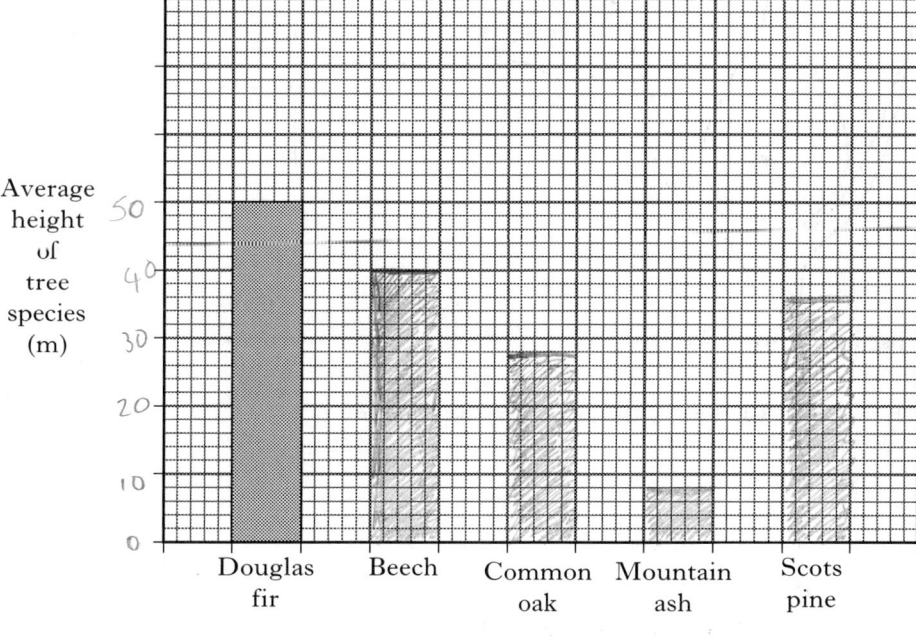

Species of tree

(2)

(ii) How many species of tree have an average height greater than that of Scots pine?

_____65_____ (1)

(iii) Calculate the ratio of the average height of a beech tree to that of a mountain ash.

Express your answer as a simple whole number ratio.

Space for calculation

Ratio _____ Beech: _____ Mountain ash (1)

(b) The diagram below shows some of the structures of a flower. Four of these structures are arrowed.

(i) The list below gives the structures and functions of some parts of the flower.

Match the correct letters to the arrows in the diagram. (2)

Letter	List
A	Stigma
B	Anther
C	Can develop into a fruit
D	Protects the unopened flower

(ii) The flower above is pollinated by insects.

Name **one** other method of pollination.

wind (1)

(iii) <u>Underline</u> one word in each set of brackets to make the sentence correct.

Pollination is the transfer of pollen from the (sepal / <u>stigma</u> / anther) to the (ovary / anther / <u>stigma</u>). (1)

(c) The diagrams below show two stages in the growth of a potato plant.

Stage A—early spring

Stage B—mid summer

(i) Name the food source used by the shoot for growth during Stage A.

_____ (1)

(ii) During Stage B, which part of the plant is making food?

_____ (1)

(iii) **Underline** one word in each set of brackets to make the sentence correct.

This method of producing potatoes is an example of $\binom{\text{asexual}}{\text{sexual}}$

reproduction and occurs by $\binom{\text{runner}}{\text{tuber}}$ formation. (1)

1995

3. (*a*) The diagram below shows part of the human digestive system.

(i) Complete the table by inserting letters from the diagram to identify the named parts of the digestive system.

Part of digestive system	Letter
Liver	~~B~~ H
Pancreas	C
Oesophagus	A
Appendix	G

(2)

(ii) Describe **one** function of the part labelled **E**.

To get rid of waste water (1)

(iii) Describe **two** features of the small intestine which help in the absorption of the products of digestion.

1. _____

2. _____ (2)

30

(b) The table below gives the percentages of different types of tissue found in the body of a typical male adult.

Body tissues	Mass (%)
Muscle	45
Bone	15
Fat (essential)	3
Fat (storage)	12
Other tissues	25

Part of this information is presented in Pie Chart 1 below.

Pie Chart 2 shows the percentages for a typical female adult.

Pie Chart 1
Typical Male Adult

Pie Chart 2
Typical Female Adult

(i) Complete Pie Chart 1, using the information from the table.
(An additional pie chart, if required, will be found on page 27.) **(2)**

(ii) Which tissue has the greatest percentage mass in both males and females?

Muscle **(1)**

(iii) Which adult contains more fat in total?

female **(1)**

(iv) A man weighs 80 kilograms. Calculate the expected mass of the muscle tissue in his body.

Space for calculation

_____ kg **(1)**

4. (*a*) The diagram below represents part of the blood circulation in a mammal. **X**, **Y** and **Z** represent blood vessels.

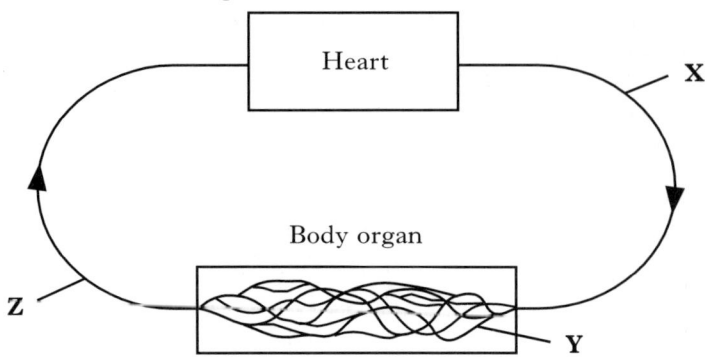

Which of the following rows A, B, C or D is correct?

Tick the correct box.

	X	Y	Z	
A	artery	vein	capillary	
B	artery	capillary	vein	
C	vein	capillary	artery	
D	vein	artery	capillary	

(1)

(*b*) The diagram below shows the site of gas exchange between a blood vessel and body cells in a mammal.

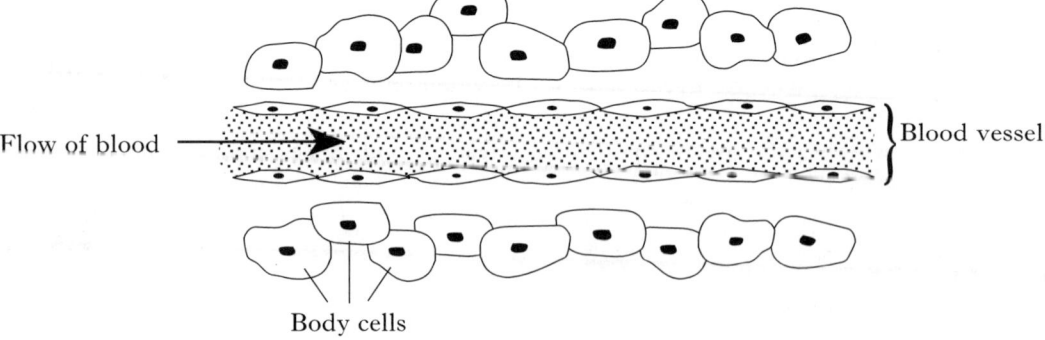

(i) Name the type of blood vessel shown.

_____ (1)

(ii) Draw an arrow on the diagram to show the direction of movement of carbon dioxide. (1)

(c) The following sentences describe the transport of gases in the blood to muscles. Use words or phrases from the list to complete the sentences. You may use each word or phrase **once**, **more than once** or **not at all**.

List
red blood cells
white blood cells
plasma
oxygen
carbon dioxide

1 Blood arriving at the muscle cells has a high concentration of

_____ and a low concentration of _____. **(1)**

2 Most of the oxygen is carried by the _____, and most

of the carbon dioxide is carried by the _____. **(2)**

(d) Decide if each of the following statements about the kidneys in a normal healthy person is **TRUE** or **FALSE**, and **tick the correct box**.

If the statement is **FALSE**, **write the correct word or phrase in the Correction box** to replace the word or phrase *underlined* in the statement.

Statement	True	False	Correction
Glucose is a waste product removed in the urine			
The kidneys regulate the *water content* of the blood.			
The ureter takes urine from the kidney to *outside the body*.			

(3)

(e) (i) The list below gives the names of some parts of the human body.

skull   nerves
heart   muscle
spinal cord   brain
backbone   lungs

Underline the **three** parts which make up the nervous system. **(1)**

(ii) Describe the function of the auditory nerve.

_____

(1)

5. (*a*) Information about three groups of micro-organisms is given below.

Group A grow well between 0 °C and 25 °C. Many of these micro-organisms cause refrigerated food to spoil.

Group B grow well between 20 °C and 45 °C. Examples in this group are micro-organisms which cause disease in humans.

Group C grow well between 45 °C and 60 °C. Compost heaps contain examples of this group.

(i) Complete the table below using the information about the three groups of micro-organisms.

Group	Temperature range suitable for growth (°C)	Site where growth of micro-organisms can occur
A		
B		Humans
C	45–60	

(ii) A fungus grows well at 27 °C. From which group does the fungus come?

Group _____

(iii) Which of the following temperatures would be suitable for the growth of two of the groups of micro-organisms?

Tick the correct box.

15 °C ☐

22 °C ☐

37 °C ☐

50 °C ☐

(b) The diagrams below show a piece of a human chromosome being transferred into a bacterial cell.

(i) What name is given to this procedure?

_____ (1)

(ii) Give an example of a product, used in medicine, which the bacterial cell can now make as a result of this transfer. State the use of this product.

Example: _____

Use: _____

_____ (2)

6. Carefully read the following passage.

Adapted from *The Scotsman*

Natural Glue

A biological glue, which may help to stop internal bleeding during surgery, has been developed in Scotland. The glue can also be spread as a thin sheet forming a natural bandage to seal a wound, while healing takes place.

5 The glue is a natural product manufactured from two blood proteins—fibrinogen and thrombin, obtained from blood plasma. When these proteins are mixed together, they form a strong clot which prevents bleeding.

The glue, because it is a natural product, acts like the body's own healing system and is eventually absorbed into the body. This gives the glue an advantage over normal surgical methods using metal staples or clips.

10 There are a whole range of opportunities for using the glue. Its main use is expected to be in surgery, where it would be used to seal leaking blood vessels and tissues. This would promote the healing of wounds and speed up recovery times for patients. Initial trials will be on patients undergoing heart surgery. The trials are necessary to confirm its safety before the glue is
15 licensed for routine use.

Answer the following questions.

(a) Name the blood proteins from which the glue is made.

fibrinogen and thrombin (1)

(b) Describe how the glue works.

_____

_____ (2)

(c) Name **one** normal surgical method of sealing wounds mentioned in the passage.

_____ (1)

(d) The glue is a natural product. State **one** advantage it has compared with normal methods of sealing wounds.

_____

_____ (1)

7. (*a*) The table below shows the volume of air breathed per minute by an athlete at rest, during exercise and during the recovery time.

Time (minutes)	Volume of air breathed per minute (litres)
0	6
2	6
4	56
6	60
8	60
10	60
12	34
14	31
16	6
18	6

(i) Complete the line graph shown on the grid below, using the information from the table.

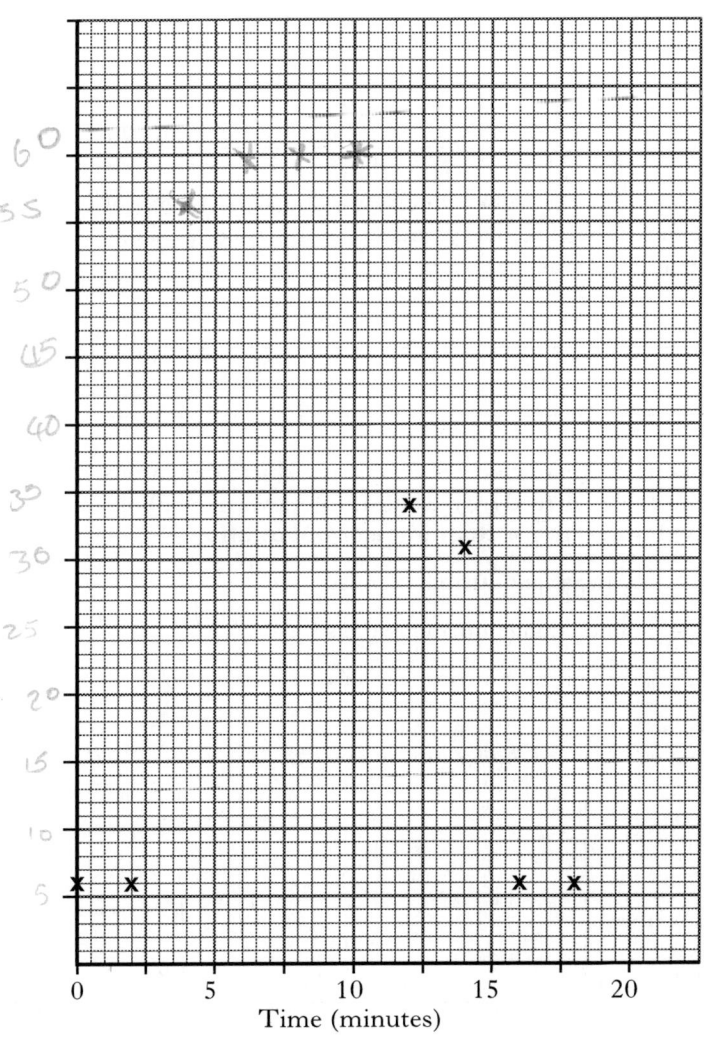

(2)

(ii) At what **time** did the athlete begin to exercise?

_____4_____ minutes (1)

(iii) During minute 2, the athlete breathed 12 times. Calculate the volume of each breath.

Space for calculation

Volume = _____ litres (1)

(iv) State the recovery time for the athlete.

Space for calculation

_____ minutes (1)

(v) Two athletes carried out the same exercise for the same length of time. Describe how their recovery times can be used to show which of the two athletes was the fitter.

_____

_____ (1)

(b) The table below contains factors which may change during vigorous exercise. Complete the table correctly by using the following symbols. Each symbol can be used **once**, **more than once** or **not at all**.

Symbols: ↑ = increases during exercise

0 = no change during exercise

↓ = decreases during exercise

Factor	Change during exercise
Lactic acid	
Pulse rate	
Carbohydrate store	
Breathing rate	

(2)

8. The apparatus drawn below was set up to demonstrate aerobic respiration.

After a few days, it was found that the level of the water had risen in the tube on Side B.

(a) Explain why small changes in room temperature during the experiment can be ignored.

_____

_____ (1)

(b) Name **two** factors which must be kept constant in the experiment.

(1) _____

(2) _____ (2)

(c) Rinsing peas in disinfectant kills micro-organisms which may grow on them. Predict what would happen to the water level in the tube on Side A if the peas were not rinsed in disinfectant. Explain your answer.

Water level _____

Explanation _____

_____

_____ (2)

9. (a) The length of the right index finger in each of a number of pupils was measured. The results are shown in the histogram below.

(i) Complete the table to display the information from the histogram.

Length of index finger (mm)	Number of pupils
40–49	6
50–59	14
60–69	25
70–79	12

(2)

(ii) What is the full range of index finger lengths shown by these pupils?

From __40__ to __79__ mm (1)

(iii) How many pupils had an index finger shorter than 70 mm?

__45__ (1)

(b) The table below gives information about a cross between pea plants of two different phenotypes.

P	F₁	F₂
red-flowered plants × white-flowered plants	all offspring have red flowers seeds of F₁ plants grown and then self-pollinated to produce F₂ offspring	5400 red-flowered plants and 1800 white-flowered plants

(i) Identify the two phenotypes used in this cross.

1. *red-flowered*   2. *white flowered*   **(1)**

(ii) Which flower colour is dominant in pea plants?

red   **(1)**

(iii) What is the ratio of red to white-flowered plants in the F₂ generation? Express your answer as a simple whole number ratio.

Space for calculation

_____ red-flowered plants : _____ white-flowered plants   **(1)**

10. (*a*) The diagrams in the table below represent parts of a pair of chromosomes in three groups of mice.

Mice	Part of pair of chromosomes	Genotype
R		BB
S		bB
T		bb

Key ● gene for black coat colour, represented by "B"

⋮ gene for brown coat colour, represented by "b"

(i) The gene for black coat colour is **dominant** to the gene for brown coat colour.

Complete the table to show the genotypes of mice S and T. (1)

(ii) Describe the phenotype(s) of the offspring of a cross between mice R and mice T.

_____

_____ (1)

(b) The following diagram shows the production of sex cells in humans. The numbers show the number of chromosomes in the cells.

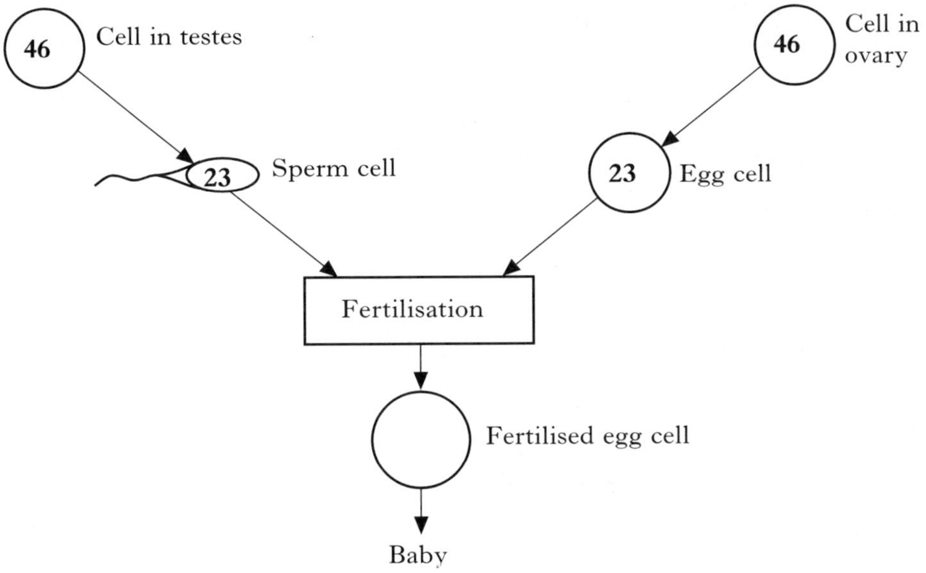

- Cell in testes (46) → Sperm cell (23)
- Cell in ovary (46) → Egg cell (23)
- Sperm cell + Egg cell → Fertilisation → Fertilised egg cell → Baby

(i) What is the general term used for sex cells?

_____ (1)

(ii) How many chromosomes will the fertilised egg cell contain?

_____ (1)

(iii) The baby inherits an X chromosome from its father.
State the sex of the baby.

_____Y_____ (1)

11. The graph below shows the relationship between temperature and hatching time for trout found in Scottish waters.

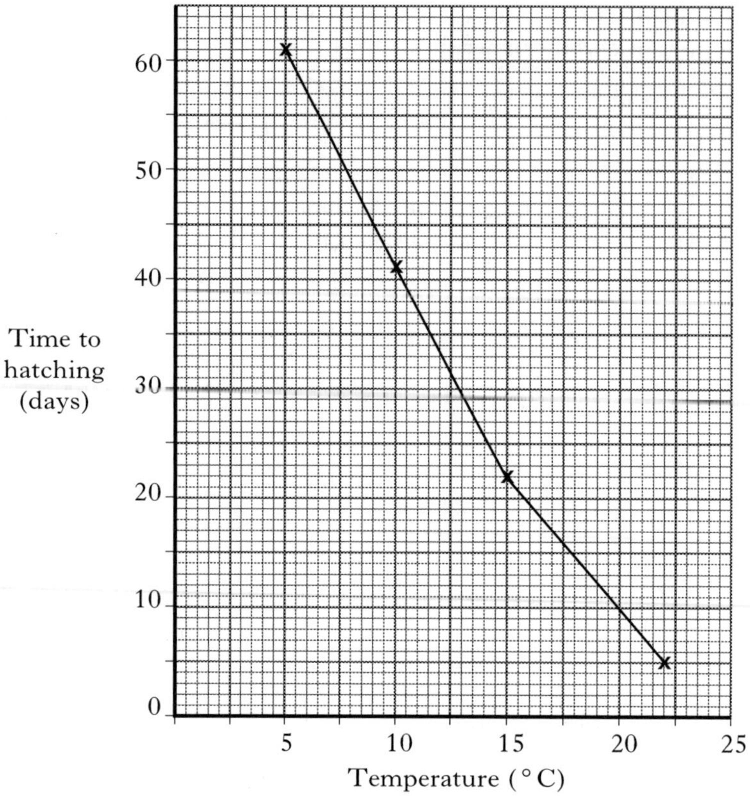

(a) State the length of time taken for the eggs to hatch at 15°C.

_____22_____ days (1)

(b) Describe the relationship between temperature and the length of time to hatching.

_____

_____ (1)

(c) Describe how fertilised trout eggs are protected until they hatch.

_____

_____ (1)

(d) Explain how trout embryos obtain their food.

_____

_____ (1)

12. (*a*) The table below refers to cell division and mitosis in a multicellular organism.

(i) **Tick one box** in each column to identify correctly features of cell division.

Function of cell division	Control of cell division	Number of chromosomes in each cell
Increases the number of cells in an organism	Cytoplasm	Twice as many as in the parent cell
Increases the size of each cell	Nucleus	Same number as in the parent cell
Allows the organism to reproduce	Cell membrane	Half as many as in the parent cell

(3)

(ii) The following diagrams show cells at different stages of mitosis.

U V W X Y

Which sequence shows the correct order of the stages?

Tick the correct box.

U → V → W → Y → X ☐

U → W → X → Y → V ☐

U → V → Y → W → X ✓

U → V → X → W → Y ☐

(1)

(b) The graph below shows changes in the number of yeast cells growing in a liquid culture medium kept at 30 °C for 24 hours.

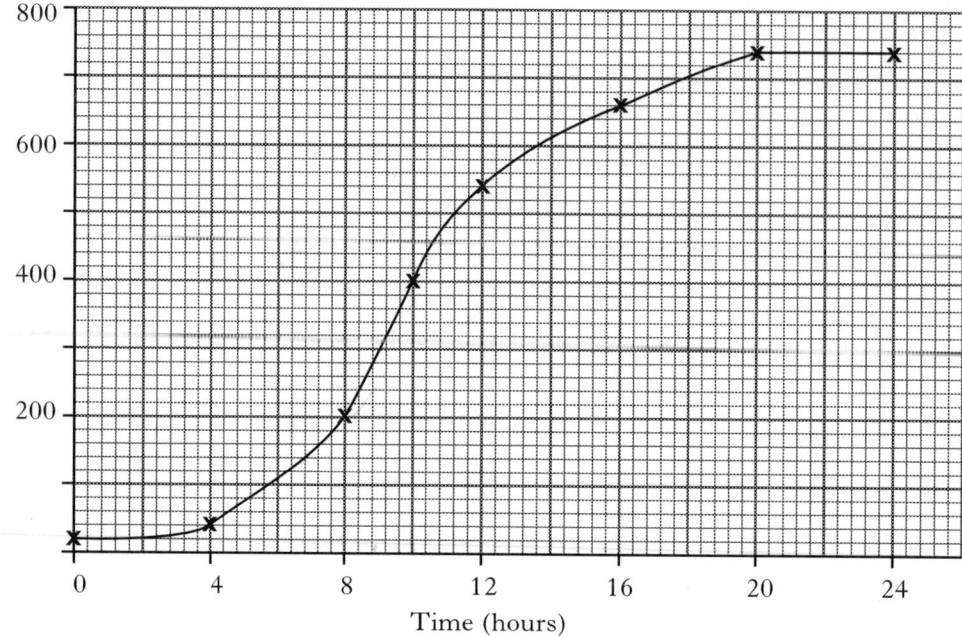

(i) During which four hour period was there the greatest increase in the number of yeast cells?

Tick the correct box.

4–8 hours ☐

8–12 hours ✓

12–16 hours ☐

16–20 hours ☐

20–24 hours ☐

(1)

(ii) State the number of hours it takes for the number of yeast cells to stop increasing and become constant.

_____20_____ hours (1)

(iii) At eight hours there are 200 million yeast cells/cm³.

How long does it take for there to be double this number?

_____10½ hours_____ hours (1)

13. Trees can be grown from berries, cuttings, nuts or seeds.

During 1994, a pupil collected the appropriate parts from the trees named in the table below.

Name of tree	Part of tree collected	Month when part collected	When the collected part is planted
Sycamore	Winged seeds	October 1994	October 1994 or Spring 1995
Chestnut	Nuts	October 1994	At time collected or Spring 1995
Aspen	Cuttings	January 1994	At time collected
Hazel	Nuts	August 1994	Spring 1995
Elder	Berries	August 1994	Spring 1996
White poplar	Cuttings	January 1994	January 1994
Ash	Winged seeds	August 1994	At time collected or Spring 1995

(a) Name a tree which can be grown from winged seeds.

Ash (1)

(b) Which tree can be grown in October 1994 from nuts?

chestnut (1)

(c) Name the part of the tree, collected in August 1994, which can be grown in both August 1994 and Spring 1995.

Ash (1)

(d) One method of artificial propagation can be found in the table.

(i) Name a tree which can be propagated artificially.

white poplar (1)

(ii) Name **one** other method of artificial propagation.

Grafting (1)

14. (a) The diagram below shows some of the structures of a typical **plant** cell.

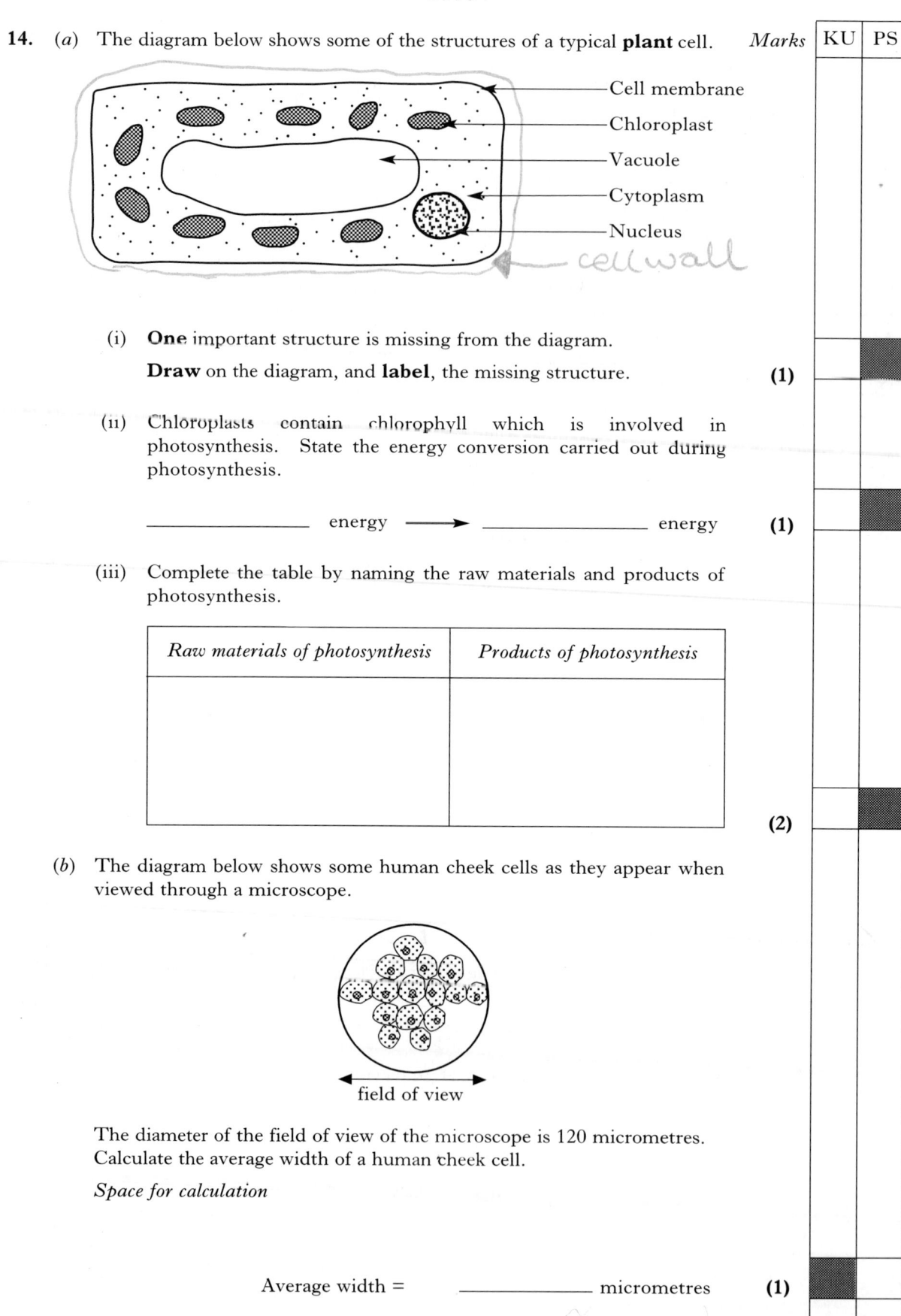

cell wall

(i) **One** important structure is missing from the diagram.

Draw on the diagram, and **label**, the missing structure. (1)

(ii) Chloroplasts contain chlorophyll which is involved in photosynthesis. State the energy conversion carried out during photosynthesis.

_____ energy ⟶ _____ energy (1)

(iii) Complete the table by naming the raw materials and products of photosynthesis.

Raw materials of photosynthesis	Products of photosynthesis

(2)

(b) The diagram below shows some human cheek cells as they appear when viewed through a microscope.

field of view

The diameter of the field of view of the microscope is 120 micrometres. Calculate the average width of a human cheek cell.

Space for calculation

Average width = _____ micrometres (1)

15. The bar chart below shows the annual rice production of a number of countries.

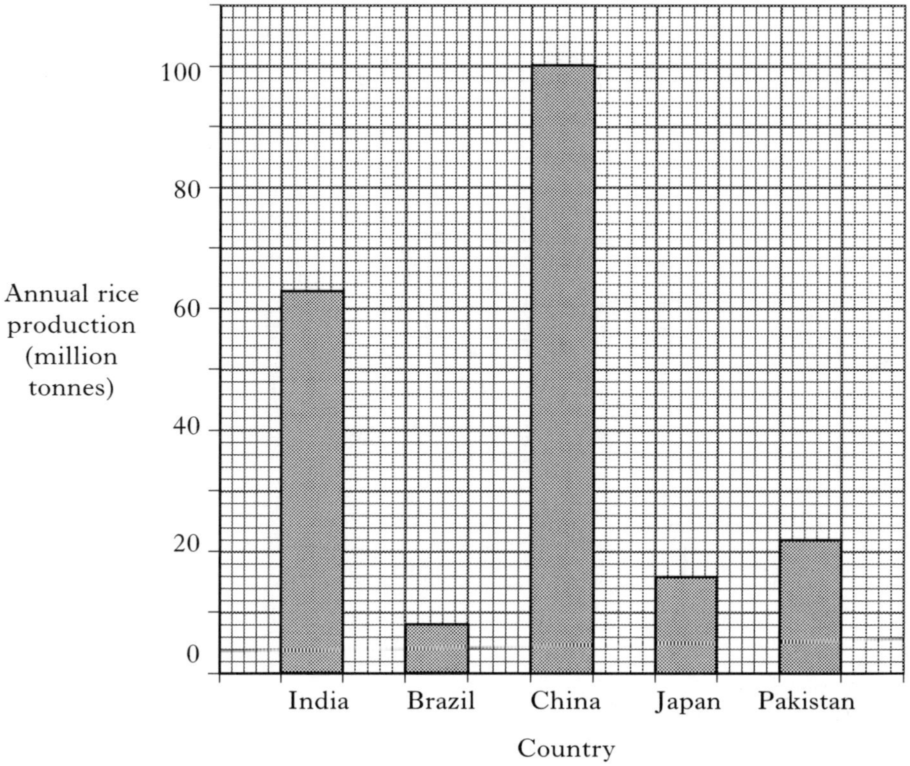

(a) What was the annual rice production of Pakistan?

_____ 22 _____ million tonnes (1)

(b) (i) The total annual world production of rice was 300 million tonnes.
Did the five named countries produce **all** this rice?
Explain your answer.

Space for calculation

_____

_____ (1)

(ii) Which country produced one third of the total annual world production of rice?

Space for calculation

_____ (1)

[*END OF QUESTION PAPER*]

SCOTTISH CERTIFICATE OF EDUCATION 1996

MONDAY, 13 MAY 9.30 AM – 11.00 AM

BIOLOGY STANDARD GRADE
General Level

Marks | KU | PS

1. The diagrams below show three different cells, not drawn to scale.

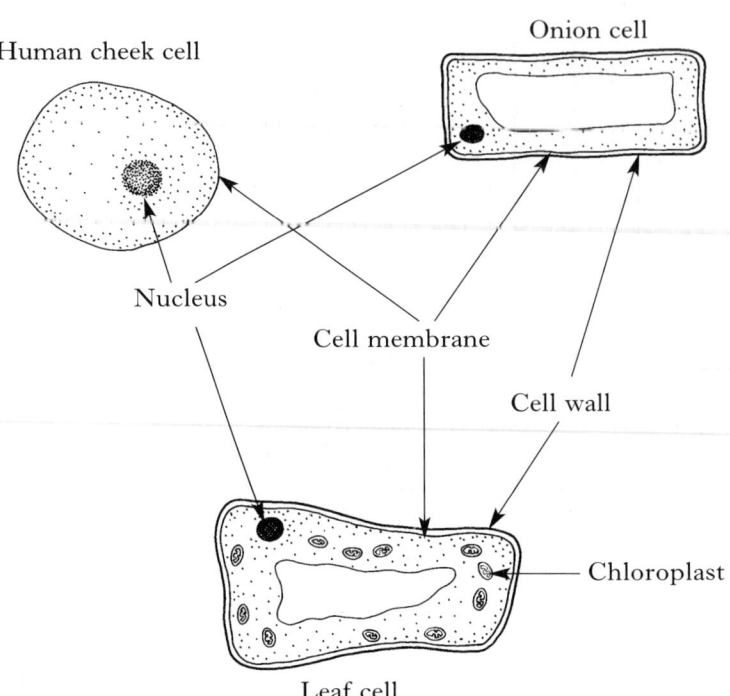

(a) Select information from the diagrams above to complete the table below. The information on the onion cell has been completed for you.

✓ = present and ✗ = absent.

Part of cell	Human cheek cell	Onion cell	Leaf cell
Nucleus		✓	
Cell membrane		✓	
Cell wall		✓	
Chloroplast		✗	

(2)

(b) Name **two** features which are found only in plant cells.

1 _____

2 _____ (1)

(c) Describe how cells can be treated so that the cell contents become more visible.

_____

_____ (1)

(d) The cell membrane **controls** the movement of substances into and out of the cell by diffusion. Name **two** substances which enter or leave the cell.

1 _____

2 _____ (2)

(e) Cells increase in number by cell division.
Name the part of the cell which controls cell division.

_____ (1)

2. (a) The diagram below shows some of the structures in the human heart.

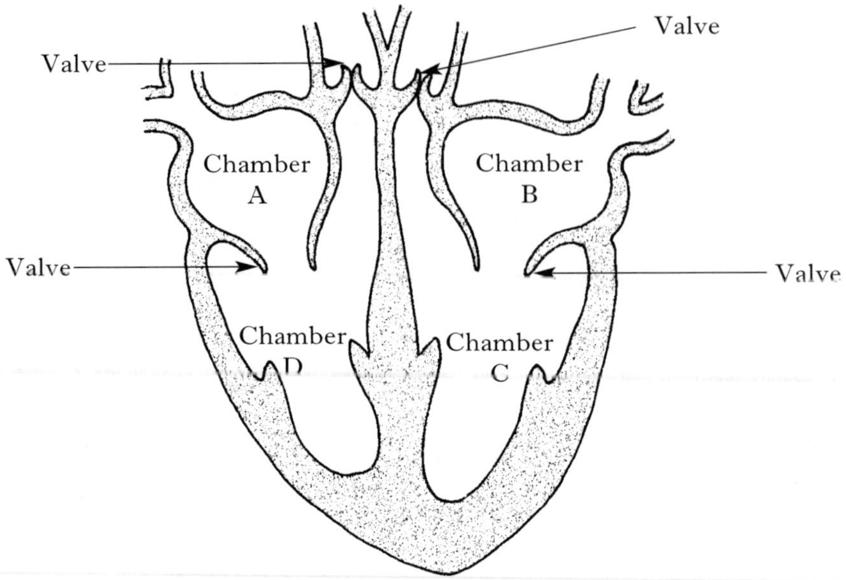

(i) **Underline** one word in each box to make the sentence correct.

Heart chamber A is the [right / left] [ventricle / atrium].

(1)

(ii) **Draw arrows on the diagram** to show the direction of blood flow into and out of chamber B.

(1)

(iii) Describe the function of the valves in the heart.

_____

_____

(1)

(iv) Explain why the wall of chamber C is thicker than the wall of chamber D.

_____

_____

(1)

(b) The diagram and statements below refer to the blood system of a mammal.

Diagram

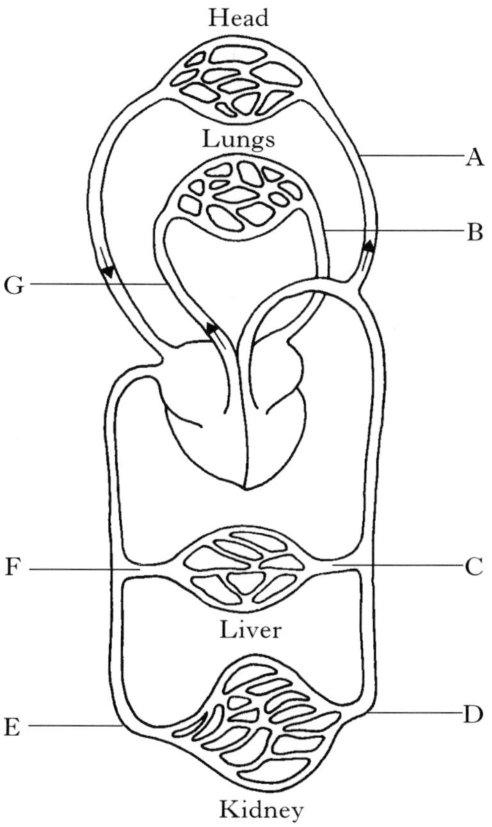

Statements

1. The **arrows** show the direction of blood flow in the blood vessel.

2. **Arteries** carry blood away from the heart towards the body organs.

3. **Veins** carry blood from the body organs back towards the heart.

(i) Write down the letters of two arteries in the diagram.

_____ and _____ are arteries. **(1)**

(ii) **Draw arrows on the diagram** to show the direction of blood flow in blood vessels **D** and **F**. **(2)**

3. (*a*) The grid below contains phrases which refer to some changes which occur during and after exercise.

A	B	C
Increase in lactic acid level	Increase in pulse rate	Increase in breathing rate
D	E	F
Decrease in lactic acid level	Decrease in pulse rate	Decrease in breathing rate

Use letters from the boxes to answer the following questions.
Each letter may be used **once, more than once or not at all**.

(i) What is the direct cause of muscle fatigue?

_____ (1)

(ii) Select **two** changes which take place in the recovery period after exercise.

_____ and _____ (2)

(b) The diagram below shows part of the excretory system of a mammal. **Complete the table** to show the names and functions of the structures labelled.

Structure	Function
	Carries blood from the kidney.
Kidney	Removes waste substances from the blood.
	Carries urine from the kidneys to the bladder.
Bladder	

(2)

(c) (i) Name a substance which is filtered from and **then reabsorbed** into the blood, in the kidney.

_____

(1)

(ii) Urine can account for 50% of all the water lost from the body. Name **one** other way in which water can be lost.

_____

(1)

4. The table below shows information about three food components in a 25 gramme packet of potato crisps.

Component	Mass (g)	Energy content (kJ/g)	Energy provided by the component in 25g crisps (kJ)
Carbohydrate	13	16	208
Protein	1	16	16
Fat	8	40	
Other	3	0	0

(a) **Complete the table** to show the energy provided by the fat in the packet of crisps.

Space for working

(1)

(b) The 25g packet of crisps contains 8g of fat.
Calculate the percentage fat in the crisps.

Space for working

Percentage fat = ———————

(1)

(c) A 25g packet of **low fat crisps** contains only 20% fat.
Calculate the mass of fat in this packet of crisps.

Space for working

Mass of fat = —————— g

(1)

5. The key below can be used to identify some flowering plants.

Key

1. Edges of leaves smooth...................................... go to 2
   Edges of leaves jagged .... go to 3

2. Heart shaped leaves .... *Wood Sorrel*
   Long narrow leaves... *Bitter Vetch*

3. Underside of leaves covered in fine hairs .... *Alpine Lady's Mantle*
   No hairs on underside of leaves.......................... go to 4

4. Leaves divided with leaf stalk .... *Wood Anemone*
   Leaves divided but without leaf stalk .... *Common Tormentil*

(a) Use the key to identify the flowering plant shown in the diagram below.

Name ———————————————— (1)

(b) Use the key to identify **two** features of Wood Anemone.

Feature 1 ————————————————————

Feature 2 ———————————————————— (2)

6. A group of pupils collected 31 leaves at random from a horse chestnut tree. They counted the number of leaflets present on each leaf.

A record of their results is shown in the table below.

Number of leaflets	Four	Five	Six	Seven
Number of leaves	׀ ׀ ׀ ׀	ⅢⅢ ⅢⅢ ⅢⅢ ⅢⅢ	ⅢⅢ	׀ ׀
Total			5	

(a) Complete the Total row in the above table. **(1)**

(b) They chose four leaves (A, B, C, and D).
Each leaf had 5 leaflets.
They measured the length of each leaflet.
A record of their results is shown in the table below.

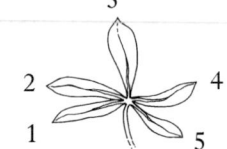

Leaf	Length of leaflet (mm)				
	Leaflet 1	Leaflet 2	Leaflet 3	Leaflet 4	Leaflet 5
A	114	175	188	160	109
B	105	137	126	124	78
C	74	98	101	87	50
D	115	162	173	169	135
Average length of leaflet (mm)		143	147	135	93

(1)

(i) **Complete the table** to show the average length of leaflet 1.

Space for working

(ii) The pupils stated that leaflet 3 was always the longest.
Identify a leaf for which this is **not** true.

Leaf _____ **(1)**

(iii) Is the length of horse chestnut leaflets an example of continuous or discontinuous variation?

_____ **(1)**

7. (*a*) The diagram below shows parts of the human female and male reproductive systems.

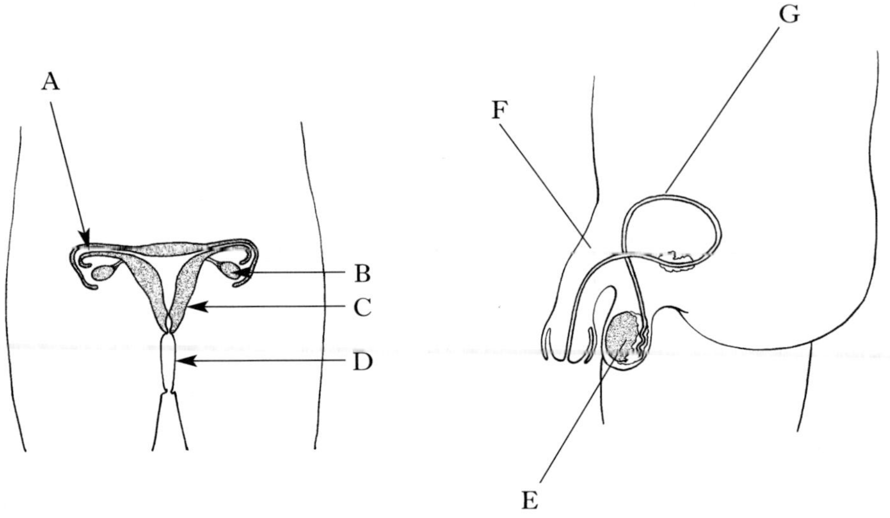

Use the letters from the diagram to answer the questions below.

(i) Where are sperm cells produced?

_____ (1)

(ii) Where does fertilisation of an egg cell take place?

_____ (1)

(iii) What is the function of structure B?

_____ (1)

(b) The table below shows the length of pregnancy for different mammals.

Mammal	Pregnancy length (weeks)
Mouse	3
Dog	9
Pig	16
Human	38
Horse	48
Elephant	84

Increasing body mass ↓

(i) Complete the bar chart below using information from the table.

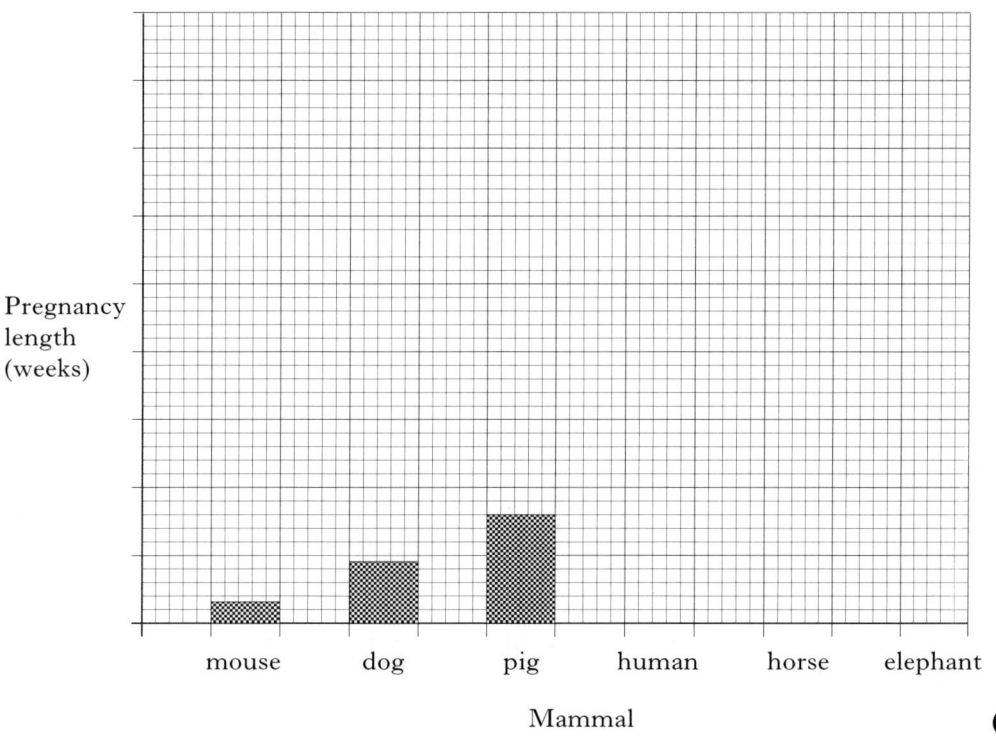

(2)

(ii) What happens to the length of pregnancy as the body mass of the mammal increases?
_____ (1)

(iii) Calculate the ratio of the length of pregnancy of the mouse to that of the elephant.
Express your answer as a simple whole number ratio.
Space for working

Ratio _____ : _____ (1)

8. The photographs below show all the chromosomes obtained from two cells. One cell was taken from person A, while the other was taken from person B.

Chromosomes from person A who has an inherited condition.

Chromosomes from person B who does not have the inherited condition.

(a) Identify the sex of the people.

_____

Explain your choice of answer.

_____ (2)

(b) The condition is caused by a chromosome mutation.

Use the information in the diagrams to identify which chromosome has undergone mutation and describe the mutation.

Chromosome mutation: Number _____ (1)

Description: _____

_____ (1)

(c) A sample of a baby's chromosomes can be obtained before birth. State the name of the technique used to obtain the cells.

_____ (1)

9. Read the passage below.

Adapted from *The Trials of Life* by David Attenborough.

Spiny lobsters are found on the coral reefs of Florida and the Bahamas. In the autumn, storms disturb the water around the reefs. The lobsters gather in large groups and begin walking in single file, each animal touching the one ahead with its long antennae. They migrate towards deeper water where they will escape the buffeting of the winter storms.

The lower temperatures in deep water will slow down their body processes so they use up less energy at a time when food is scarce. Their navigation system may simply detect cooler water. They may also be able to detect the direction of wave movements.

Moving in single file reduces the drag of the water on all but the leader. Moving this way also allows them to respond quickly if they are attacked by trigger fish. They form defensive circles with their pincers pointing outwards.

Answer the questions based on the passage.

(a) What makes the lobsters begin to migrate?

_____ (1)

(b) Describe how each lobster keeps its place in the migrating group.

_____

_____ (1)

(c) Give **one** reason why moving into colder water is an advantage to the lobsters.

_____

_____ (1)

(d) State an advantage to the lobsters of moving in single file.

_____ (1)

(e) The passage describes an example of rhythmical behaviour—migration in spiny lobsters.

Describe **one** other example of rhythmical behaviour and state the external trigger stimulus.

Rhythmical behaviour _____ (1)

Trigger stimulus _____ (1)

10. (*a*) The information in the boxes below refers to parts of the skeleton and to organs in the body.

Part(s) of the skeleton   *Organ(s) in the body*

Vertebrae		Brain
Skull		Heart and lungs
Rib cage		Spinal cord

(i) **Use arrows** to join the boxes on the left with those on the right, so that the part of the skeleton which **protects** each of the body organs is shown correctly.

(2)

(ii) The skeleton protects body organs.
State one **other** function of the skeleton.

_____

(1)

(*b*) Decide if each of the following statements about joints is **TRUE** or **FALSE** and **tick the appropriate box**.

If you tick the **FALSE box you must write the correct word or words in the Correction box** to replace the word(s) *underlined* in the statement.

Statement	True	False	Correction
A hinge joint allows movement in *every direction*			
Ligaments attach muscles to bones			
Cartilage reduces friction at a joint			

(3)

11. The graph below shows the rate of water loss from leaves over a 24 hour period.

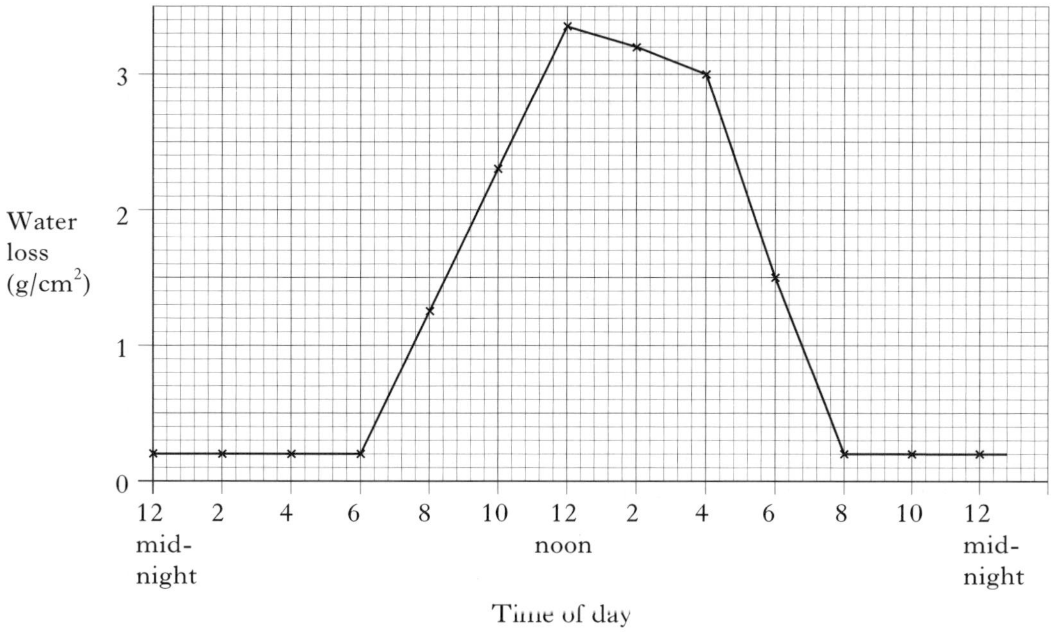

(a) (i) What is the highest rate of water loss during the 24 hour period?

_____ g/cm^2 (1)

(ii) The rate of water loss increases from its lowest value to its highest value in 6 hours.
How long does it take to fall from its highest value back down to its lowest value?

_____ hours (1)

(b) (i) Leaf surfaces contain pores through which water vapour is lost.
Name these pores.

_____ (1)

(ii) Name **one other** substance that passes into or out of the leaf through these pores.

_____ (1)

12. A group of pupils carried out some survey work on a freshwater pond over a period of time.

The results in the table below show some of their findings.

Temperature of water (°C)	Oxygen concentration (mg/l)
0	15
10	13
15	12
20	10
25	8

(a) On the grid below, complete the axes and plot a line graph to show the effect of temperature on the oxygen concentration found in the water.

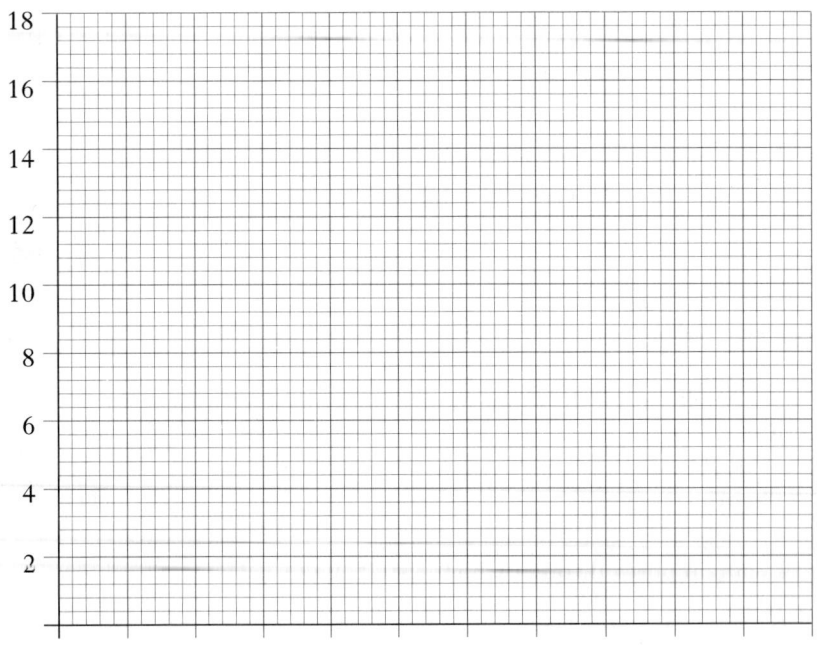

Temperature of water (°C)

(3)

(b) Describe the relationship between the temperature of the water and the oxygen concentration.

_____

_____ (1)

(c) The pupils also sampled organisms in the pond and used books to find out their feeding relationships.

"Pond snails, shrimps, mayfly larvae and stonefly larvae feed on weeds and plant plankton in the pond. The shrimps are eaten by water beetles. The water beetles are eaten by minnows and sticklebacks. The pond snails are eaten by leeches which in turn are eaten by trout."

(i) The arrows in a food chain show the direction of energy flow.

Use the information in the passage to complete the food chain below.

_____ → pond snails → _____ → _____ (1)

(ii) Name **two** organisms that are in competition with each other for the same food.

_____ and _____ (1)

(iii) Some organisms in the pond are producers and others are consumers.

Describe what is meant by each of the terms.

Producer

_____

_____ (1)

Consumer

_____

_____ (1)

13. An investigation was carried out to compare the catalase content in a variety of tissues. Catalase is an enzyme found in living cells; it breaks down hydrogen peroxide into water and oxygen.

A cube of potato tissue was added to some hydrogen peroxide.

The volume of oxygen released during the next 3 minutes was collected and measured as shown below.

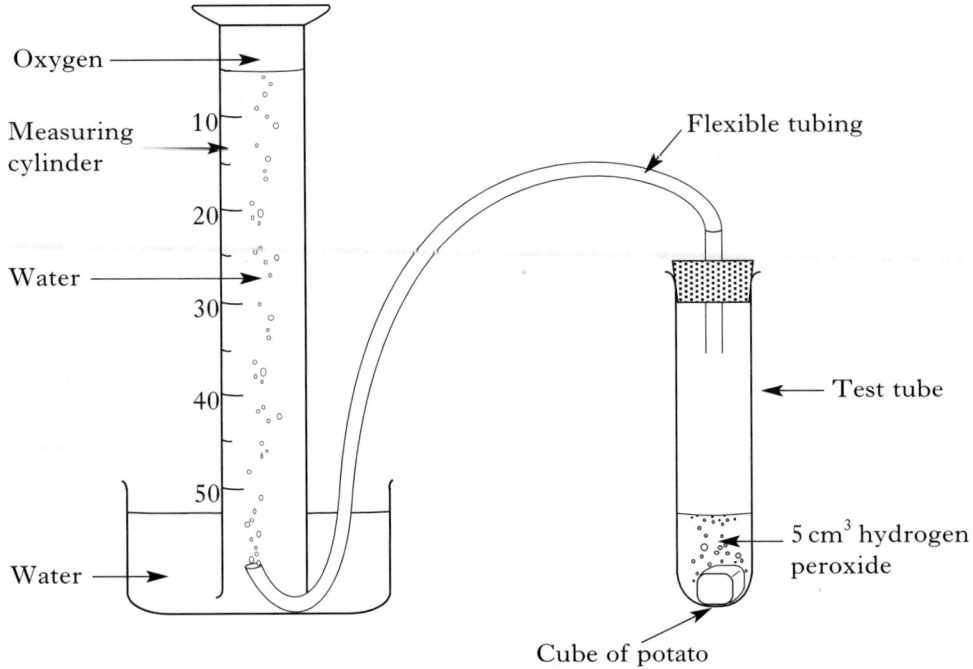

The experimental method was repeated using cubes of liver, apple and carrot. The results are shown in the table below.

Tissue	Volume of oxygen collected in 3 minutes (cm^3)
Potato	5·0
Liver	39·5
Apple	0·5
Carrot	3·0

(a) (i) Which tissue contains the least catalase?

_____ (1)

(ii) Which tissue contains the most catalase?

_____ (1)

(b) Name **two** factors (not connected with the apparatus) which must be kept constant to ensure that a valid comparison of the catalase content of the tissues can be made.

1 _____

2 _____ (2)

(c) Briefly describe a suitable control for the experiment.

_____

_____ (1)

(d) Explain why several samples of each tissue should have been used and an average volume of oxygen calculated.

_____

_____ (1)

(e) Another plant tissue which contains catalase was used in the experiment. It contains more catalase than carrot but less than potato. Predict the volume of oxygen which would be collected in 3 minutes.

It would be more than _____ cm^3, but less than _____ cm^3. (1)

14. Paper can be made more cheaply from recycled waste paper than directly from wood pulp.

The bar chart below shows the percentage of recycled paper fibre used in the manufacture of paper materials in the UK in 1992.

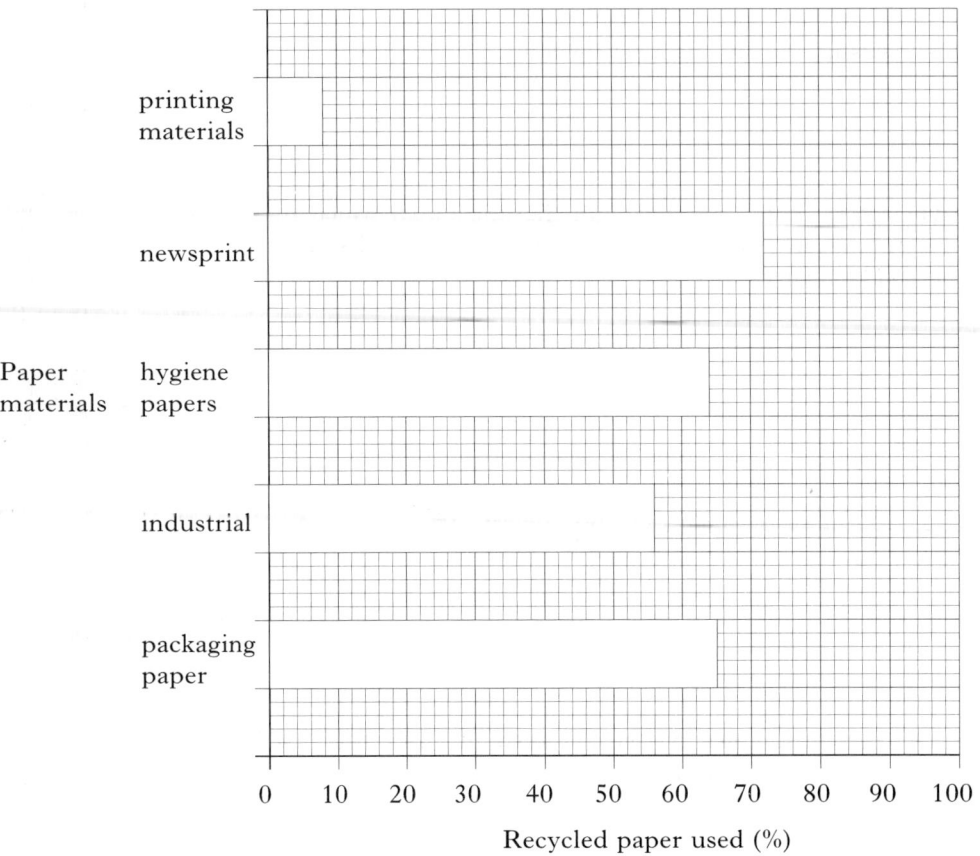

(a) Use the information in the bar chart to complete the table below.

printing materials	8
newsprint	
hygiene papers	64
industrial	56
packaging paper	

(3)

(b) The average family throws 5 kilogrammes of waste paper into the dustbin each week.

Calculate how long it would take for the average family to discard 90 kilogrammes of waste paper.

Space for calculation

_____ weeks (1)

(c) The manufacture of paper from wood pulp is an example of a use of plants.

Describe **two** other uses of plants.

1 _____

2 _____ (2)

(d) The paper industry used to be associated with pollution.
Name **one** other source of pollution.

_____ (1)

15. Seed colour in pea plants is genetically controlled.

Generation A: True-breeding white pea seeds × True-breeding grey-brown pea seeds

All seeds are grey-brown in colour
Only these seeds were used in the cross below

Generation B: Grey-brown pea seeds × Grey-brown pea seeds

Generation C: 25 white pea seeds, 75 grey-brown pea seeds

(a) Which **column** in the table below correctly identifies generations A, B and C?

Tick the correct box.

	Symbol for generation			
Generation A	P	F_2	P	F_1
Generation B	F_2	F_1	F_1	P
Generation C	F_1	P	F_2	F_2

(1)

(b) Which seed colour is dominant?

_____

(c) Complete the table below by placing a tick or a cross in each box to show which seeds are true-breeding.

✓ = true-breeding   ✗ = not true-breeding

	Seed colour	True-breeding
Generation A	White	
Generation A	Grey-brown	
Generation B	Grey-brown	
Generation C	White	

(d) In generation C there were 25 white pea seeds and 75 grey-brown pea seeds.

Complete the pie chart below to display this information.

Key

☐ White seeds

▦ Grey-brown seeds

16. (*a*) The grid below refers to micro-organisms and the production of food and drink.

A Bacterium	B Single-celled	C Carbon dioxide	D Alcohol
E Oxygen	F Sugar	G Fungus	H Multi-celled

Use letters from the boxes to answer the following questions.
Each letter may be used **once, more than once or not at all**.

(i) Which **two** terms are used to describe yeast?

_____ and _____ (2)

(ii) Which **two** products are formed during the fermentation of glucose?

_____ and _____ (2)

(iii) Which substance, produced by yeast, is responsible for the raising of dough?

_____ (1)

(iv) Which type of micro-organism is used in the production of yoghurt?

_____ (1)

(b) The graph below shows the growth of a population of bacteria used to produce a type of single cell protein. The bacteria were grown at a constant temperature of 35 °C.

No of bacteria/cm^3 vs Time (hours)

(i) How many bacteria were present at 25 hours?

_____ cm^3 **(1)**

(ii) State **one** factor which could have been limiting the growth of the population at point C on the graph.

_____ **(1)**

(iii) **Tick the correct box** to show the relationship at point B on the graph.

The number of new bacteria is equal to the number dying. ☐

The number of new bacteria is greater than the number dying. ☐

The number of new bacteria is less than the number dying. ☐ **(1)**

17. Gros Michel is a variety of banana plant.

To try to improve the Gros Michel variety, plant breeders crossed it with another type of banana plant. This banana plant had good resistance to Panama disease and leaf spot disease.

The table below shows the characteristics of Gros Michel and the new variety of banana.

Characteristic of the banana plant	Gros Michel	New Variety
Produces large bunches of fruit	yes	no
Possesses resistance to Panama disease	no	yes
Produces fruit containing no seeds	yes	yes
Possesses resistance to leaf spot disease	no	no

(a) Which **two** characteristics does Gros Michel lack?

1 _____

2 _____ (1)

(b) Suggest **two** reasons why plant breeders considered the new variety to be an unsuccessful product from the above cross?

Reason 1 _____

_____

Reason 2 _____

_____ (2)

[*END OF QUESTION PAPER*]

SCOTTISH CERTIFICATE OF EDUCATION 1997

MONDAY, 12 MAY
9.30 AM – 11.00 AM

BIOLOGY
STANDARD GRADE
General Level

Marks

1. (a) A group of pupils carried out an investigation on the light intensity 0·5m above the ground in areas A and B shown in the diagram below.

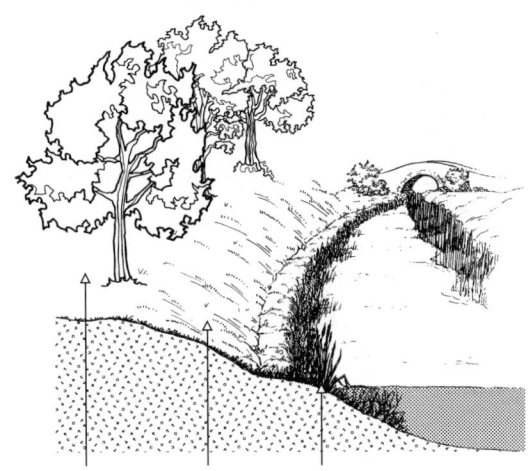

Area A   Area B   Area C

Five readings were taken at 12 noon on the same day in each area. The results are shown in the table below.

	Light reading (Units)	
	Area A	Area B
	4	20
	5	22
	3	19
	4	19
	4	20
Average	4	20

(i) Give **one** reason why the average reading for Area A was lower than that for Area B.

_____

_____ (1)

(ii) Name an abiotic factor, other than light intensity, which may have been responsible for different plants growing in Area C, as distinct from Areas A and B.

_____ (1)

(b) Complete the table below by supplying the missing words.

Word	Meaning
	The place where an organism lives
Population	A group of organisms of the same species living in the same area
	All the organisms living in a particular area

(2)

(c) The diagram below shows part of a food web in a Scottish loch.

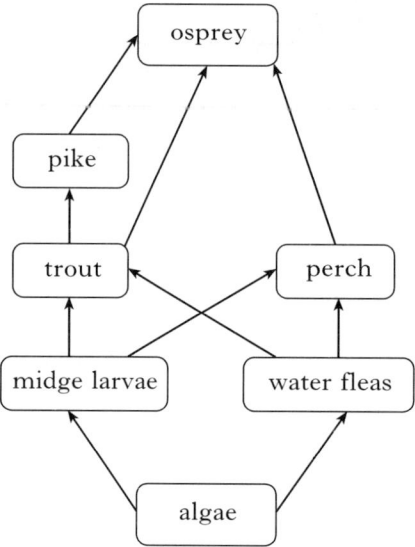

(i) Name the producer in this food web.

_____ (1)

(ii) Select an example of a complete food chain consisting of four organisms from the food web above.

_____ → _____ → _____ → _____ (1)

(iii) Not all the energy in a food web becomes available as energy for the next level. Give **one** way in which energy is lost from a food web.

_____ (1)

2. (*a*) The diagram below shows the lower surface of a green leaf, together with a small area of the surface as seen through a microscope.

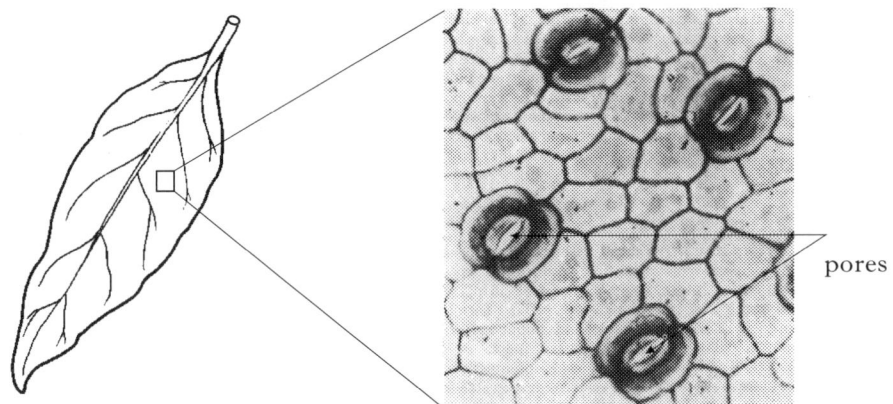

(i) Plant leaves have pores which can open and close, through which water is lost.

Name these pores.

_____ (1)

(ii) Which gas, needed for photosynthesis, **enters** the plant through these pores?

_____ (1)

(*b*) Some of the characteristics of six related British plants are shown in the table.

Species	Thorns	Flower colour	Number of petals
Pear	no	white	five
Silverweed	no	yellow	five
Trailing Rose	yes	white	five
Dog Rose	yes	white tinged with pink	five
Crab Apple	no	white tinged with pink	five
Common Tormentil	no	yellow	four

(i) Use the information in the table to complete the key below. Write a name or a characteristic into each empty box.

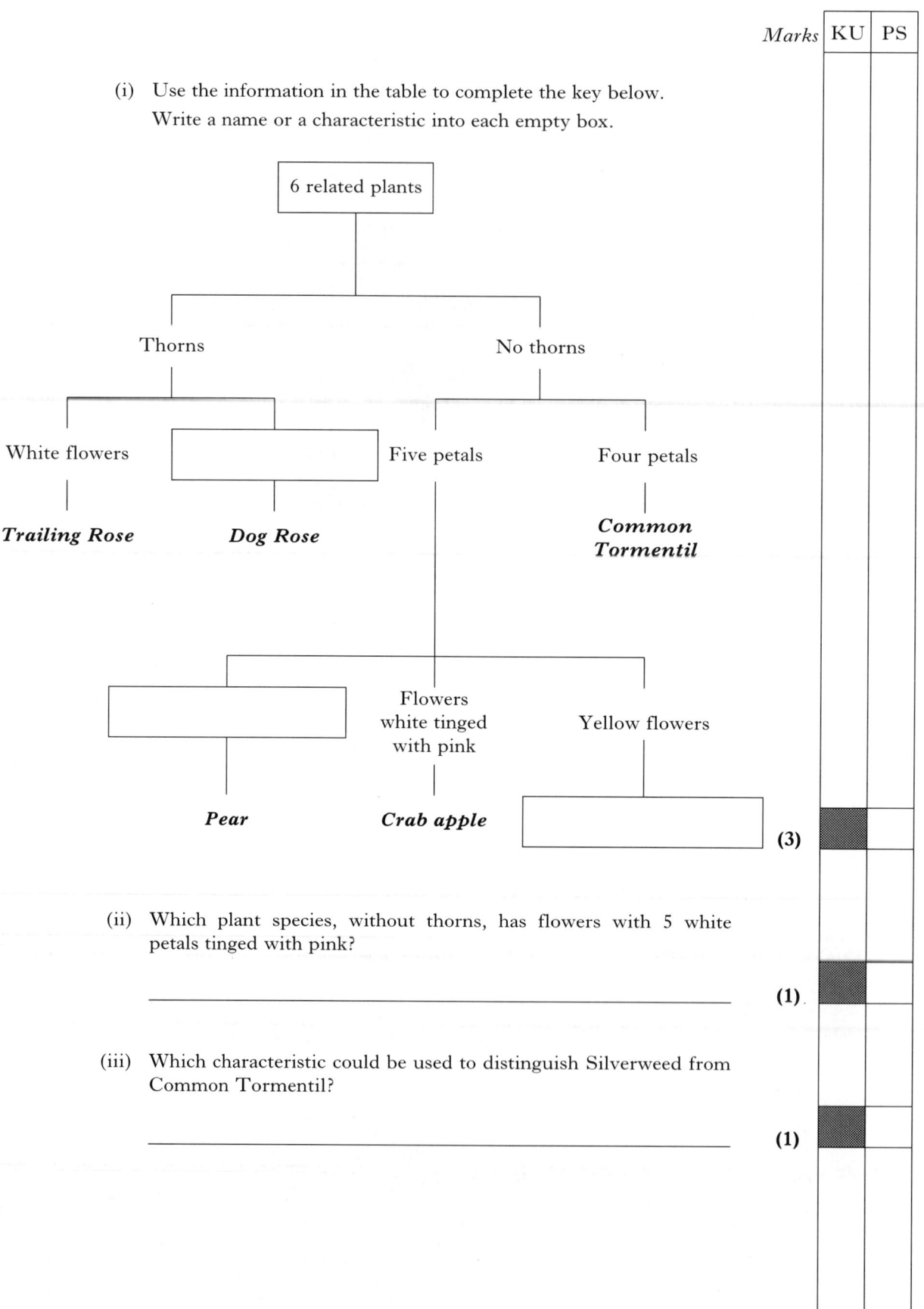

(3)

(ii) Which plant species, without thorns, has flowers with 5 white petals tinged with pink?

_____ (1)

(iii) Which characteristic could be used to distinguish Silverweed from Common Tormentil?

_____ (1)

3. The diagram below represents a section through a seed.

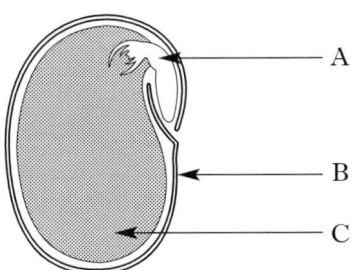

(a) Complete the table by writing the letter, name or function of each structure.

Letter	Name of structure	Function
B	Seed coat	Tough protective outer covering
		Source of energy and raw materials
	Embryo	

(2)

(b) The graph below shows the yield of wheat when the number of seeds sown per square metre was increased.

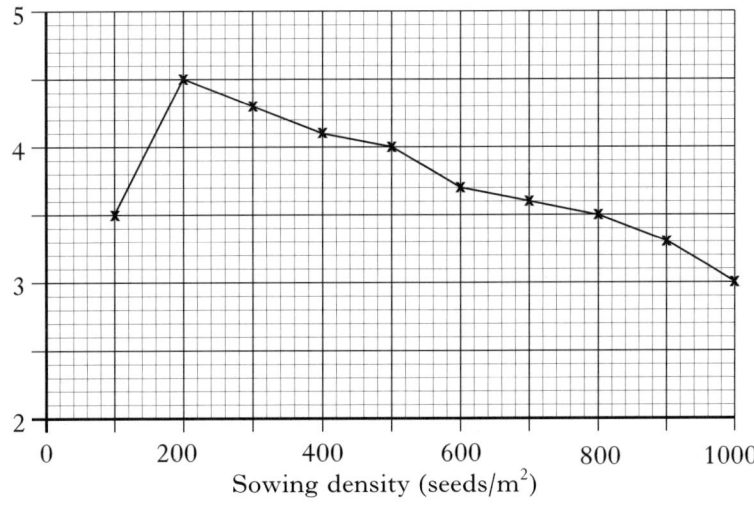

(i) State the number of seeds sown per square metre which gave the maximum yield.

_____ seeds per m^2

(1)

(ii) When 800 seeds per square metre were sown, the yield was only 3·5 kg/m². Suggest a reason for this lower yield.

_____

_____ (1)

(c) The table below shows world crop production in 1970 and 1992.

Crop	Production (million tonnes)	
	1970	1992
Wheat	264	511
Maize	219	457
Potatoes	275	285
Vegetables	202	421
Citrus fruits	140	326
Total	1100	2000

(i) Name the crop which had the highest production in 1992.

_____ (1)

(ii) Which crop shows the greatest increase in production between 1970 and 1992?

_____ (1)

(iii) Calculate the production of potatoes in 1970 as a percentage of the total crop production in that year.

Space for working

_____ % (1)

4. Fibre is an important part of a healthy diet.

   The fibre content of some vegetables is given in the table below.

Vegetable	Fibre content (%)
Brussels sprouts	2
Peas	52
Spinach	63
Carrots	26
Sweetcorn	40
Beans	15

   (a) On the grid below, **complete the axis and bars** to show the fibre content of each of the vegetables.

   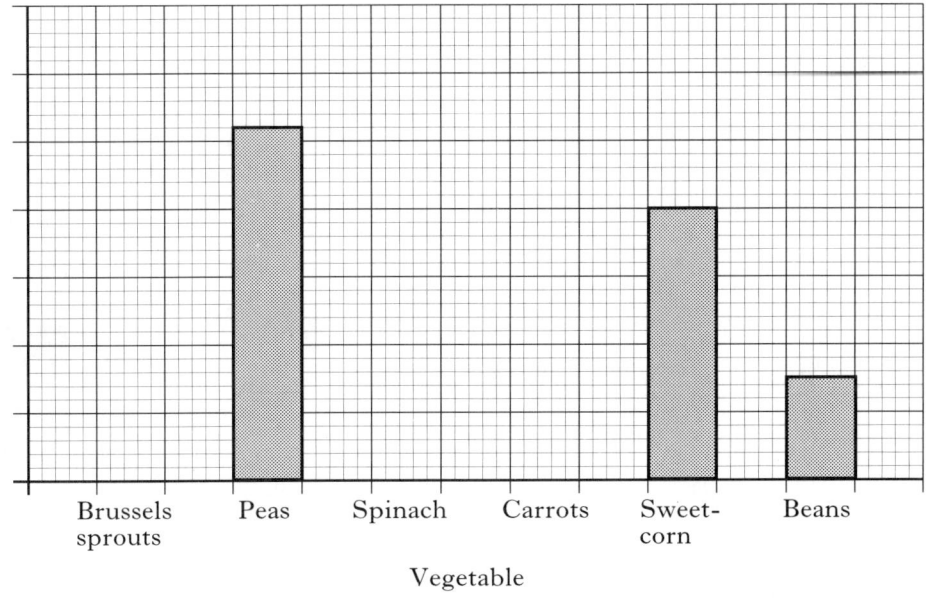

   (2)

   (b) Some vegetables are better sources of dietary fibre than others. Which vegetables have a fibre content greater than 30%?

   _____

   (1)

(c) Calculate the whole number ratio of fibre in peas to that in carrots.

Space for working

Ratio _____ : _____   (1)

       fibre in peas : fibre in carrots

(d) Calculate the number of grammes of fibre present in a 50 g portion of sweetcorn.

Space for working

_____ g   (1)

5. (*a*) The diagram below shows some of the parts of the human digestive system.

   (i) Complete the table by entering letters from the diagram to identify the named parts of the digestive system.

Part of digestive system	Letter
Gall bladder	
Rectum	
Stomach	
Small intestine	

   (2)

   (ii) State **one** function of the large intestine.

   _____ (1)

(*b*) Teeth are involved in the mechanical breakdown of food.
   Describe the role of the following teeth in a **herbivore.**

   Incisor _____ (1)

   Molar _____ (1)

(c) The diagram below shows part of the urinary system.

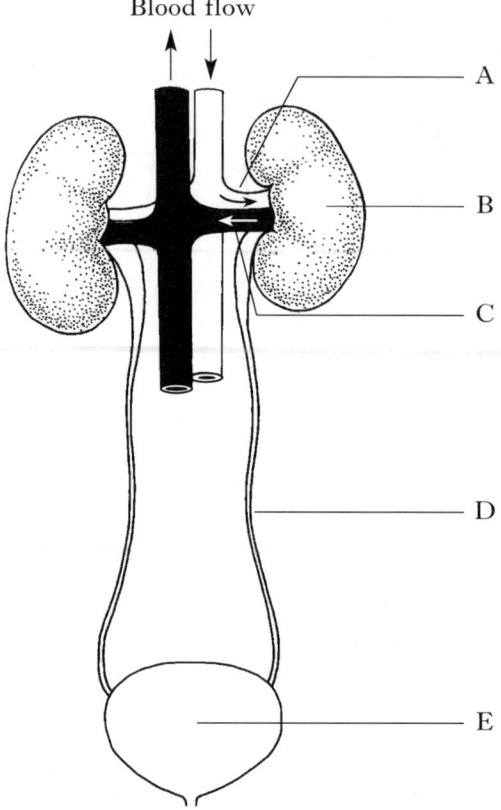

Decide if each of the following statements is **TRUE** or **FALSE** and **tick the appropriate box**.

If the statement is **FALSE, write the correct word in the Correction box** to replace the word *underlined* in the statement.

Statement	True	False	Correction
Structure C is the renal *artery*			
Structure D carries *blood* from the kidney			
Structure E stores *urine*			

(3)

6. (*a*) The grid below contains the names of structures in the reproductive system of mammals.

A	B	C	D
Uterus	Oviduct	Amniotic sac	Ovary

Use the letters from the grid to identify the structure

(i) where fertilisation occurs _____ **(1)**

(ii) which contains fluid to support the embryo. _____ **(1)**

(*b*) The diagram below shows a sample being taken from the fluid which surrounds a fetus. The fluid contains cells from the fetus which are examined for chromosome abnormalities.

(i) Name the procedure described above.

_____ **(1)**

(ii) Cells from the fetus were found to contain an extra chromosome. Name a condition caused by a chromosome mutation.

_____ **(1)**

(iii) The fetus receives food through structure X. State the source of this food.

_____ **(1)**

7. (a) The diagram below shows a human heart.

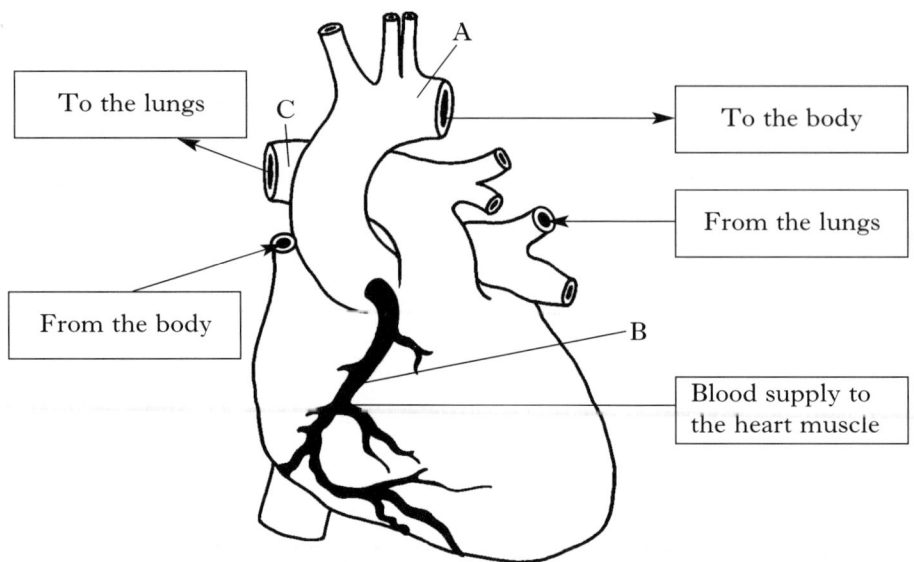

Complete the table below to show whether the blood in vessels A, B and C is oxygenated (high oxygen concentration) or deoxygenated (low oxygen concentration) by placing a tick in the correct column.

Vessel	Oxygenated blood	Deoxygenated blood
A		
B		
C		

(2)

(b) Describe the function of each of the following.

1 Red blood cells _____

_____ (1)

2 Plasma _____

_____ (1)

8. A pupil carried out the following investigation into the feeding of caterpillars.

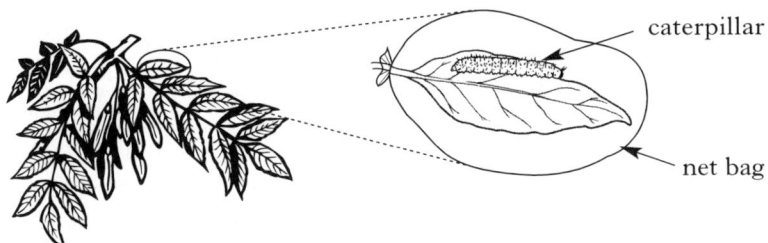

Each day, the mass of the caterpillar was measured.
The results are shown in the table below.

Time from start (days)	Mass of caterpillar (mg)
0	5000
1	5300
2	5600
3	5800
4	6000
5	6200
6	6200

(a) (i) On the grid below, **complete both axes and draw a line graph** to show the mass of the caterpillar during the time of the investigation.

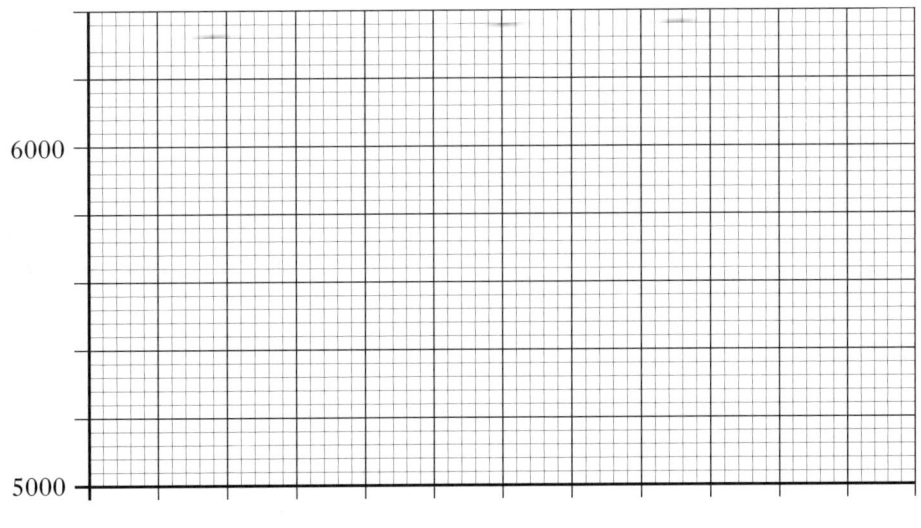

(3)

(ii) Calculate the average daily increase in mass of the caterpillar.

Space for working

Average daily increase in mass _____ mg **(1)**

(b) Each day the area of leaf which remained uneaten was measured.

Time from start (days)	Area of leaf uneaten (mm²)
0	140
1	125
2	110
3	95
4	90
5	80
6	70

Calculate the percentage of the original leaf area **which had been eaten by the caterpillar** by the end of the investigation.

Space for working

_____% **(1)**

(c) Explain why the net bag was placed around the leaf and the caterpillar.

_____

_____ **(1)**

9. (a) Match each of the descriptions below with a word from the list by writing the word in the box.

Description	Word
A group of organisms which can breed together and produce fertile offspring.	
Slight differences which occur between individual organisms of the same type.	

List
Community
Mutations
Genotypes
Species
Variations

(2)

(b) A true-breeding fruit fly with normal wings was crossed with a true-breeding fruit fly which had vestigial wings. All the offspring had normal wings.

Two of these offspring were crossed together and the next generation contained normal winged and vestigial winged flies.

These crosses are shown in the diagram below.

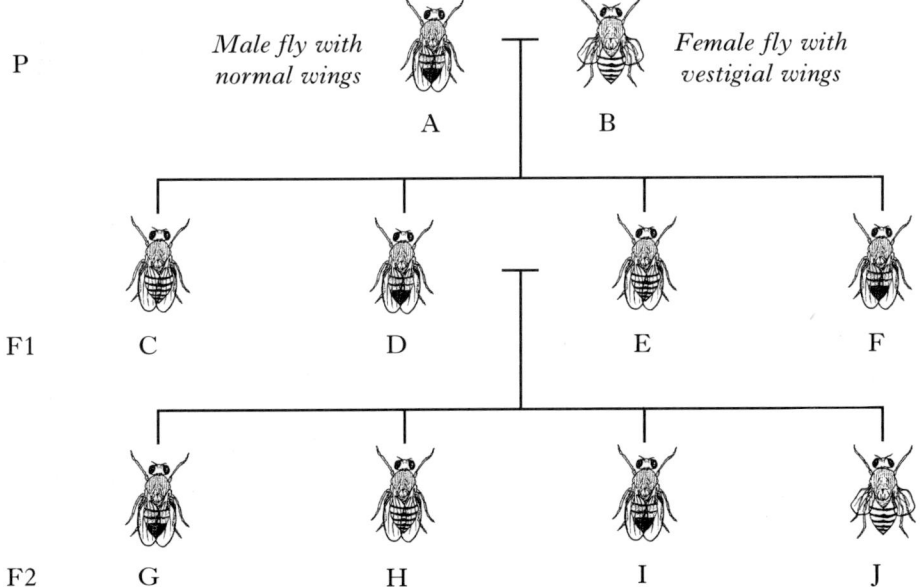

P — A Male fly with normal wings × B Female fly with vestigial wings

F1 — C, D, E, F

F2 — G, H, I, J

Use the letters from the diagram to answer the following questions.

(i) Identify **two** flies from **different generations** which have the same phenotype.

Fly _____ and Fly _____

Describe that phenotype.

_____

(1)

(ii) State the dominant characteristic of the flies used in these crosses.

_____

(1)

(iii) From the parental and first generation only, identify **two** flies which have the same phenotype but different genotypes.

Fly _____ and Fly _____

(1)

10. (a) The diagram below represents a plant cell as seen under a microscope.

nucleus

cell wall

(i) Complete each box with the name of the labelled structure. **(2)**

(ii) What is the function of the nucleus?

_____ **(1)**

(iii) From the diagram, select **one** piece of evidence to confirm that this is a plant cell.

_____ **(1)**

(b) The diagrams below show some human cheek cells as they appeared under a microscope, at two different magnifications.

×100   ×200

Describe the effect that increasing the magnification had on

(i) the apparent size of the cells

_____ **(1)**

(ii) the area of the slide seen.

_____ **(1)**

(c) Name the process by which small soluble molecules can enter or leave cells.

_____ **(1)**

11. Use the information in the table below to answer the following questions about the simple aquatic organisms. Each organism consists of a single cell.

Appearance (not drawn to scale)	Average cell length (mm)	Features
Amoeba (diagram showing food vacuole, water vacuole, nucleus, jelly like surface)	1	Move by making the cytoplasm flow in any direction. Feed by flowing round smaller organisms
Euglena (diagram showing membrane, eye spot, water vacuole, nucleus, flagellum, chloroplast)	0·1	Move by a whipping action of the long flagellum. Make food by photosynthesis
Paramecium (diagram showing food vacuole, membrane, nucleus, gullet, cilia, water vacuole)	0·2	Move by rhythmical beating of rows of cilia. Feed by taking food particles into the gullet and then into the cytoplasm

(a) Which organism has the smallest cells? _____ (1)

(b) Which organism does not contain food vacuoles? _____ (1)

(c) Which organism moves using cilia? _____ (1)

(d) *Euglena* carries out photosynthesis. Describe **one** way in which *Euglena* differs from typical green plant cells.

_____ (1)

12. (a) The diagram below shows a cell during mitosis.

   (i) Which of the following diagrams represents the cell during the next stage of mitosis?

   Tick the correct box.

   (1)

   (ii) How many chromosomes would be found in the body cells of the organism from which this cell was taken?

   Number of chromosomes _____

   (1)

(b) The following statements refer to mitosis.
   A   Chromosomes are visible during mitosis.
   B   Mitosis only occurs in plants.
   C   Mitosis halves the number of chromosomes in the new cells.
   D   Mitosis increases the number of cells.

   Identify the true statement(s) by writing the appropriate letter(s) in the box below.

True Statement(s)	

   (1)

(c) A bean seed germinated and grew a root.

The root was marked with waterproof ink at 3 mm intervals.

The diagrams below show the bean when it was first marked and 48 hours later.

Start   After 48 hours

(i) What was the increase in the root length during the 48 hours after it was marked?

Root growth _____ mm

(1)

(ii) Which **one** of the following statements correctly describes the growth of the bean root.

Tick the correct box.

Growth takes place equally along the length of the root. ☐

Growth takes place at the tip of the root. ☐

Growth takes place in a region immediately behind the root tip. ☐

Growth takes place from the part of the root nearest to the bean. ☐

(1)

13. Read the following passage carefully.

Adapted from *Algal Blooms in Scottish Lochs* from Data Support, WWF Scotland/Scottish Natural Heritage

Loch Leven is a very important National Nature Reserve. It has the biggest concentration of breeding ducks in Britain and up to 40 000 waterbirds of various kinds visit it each winter.

The loch is naturally rich in nutrients such as phosphate and nitrates, but the levels have been increased because of human activity in the surrounding area. One result has been the appearance of massive blue-green algal blooms in summer. These are composed of microscopic plants which multiply rapidly and turn the water a deep green colour. These microscopic plants release poisonous chemicals when they die and decompose.

The key nutrient in producing an algal bloom is phosphate. Phosphates enter the loch in discharges from a local woollen mill, in domestic sewage and in run-off from the surrounding farmland.

Following a particularly intense algal bloom in 1992, the woollen mill further reduced the phosphates in its discharges and the sewage works installed equipment to remove phosphates from the water it discharged into the loch. Controls have also been imposed on housing development in the area to ensure that phosphate from domestic sewage remains at low levels.

Answer the questions.

(a) Why is Loch Leven Nature Reserve an important site?

_____ (1)

(b) What caused the outbreaks of algal blooms in the loch?

_____ (1)

(c) Why were efforts made to prevent the formation of algal blooms?

_____ (1)

(d) Name **two** sources of the phosphate pollution in Loch Leven.

1 _____

2 _____ (2)

(e) Describe **one** way in which phosphate from domestic sewage is being controlled.

_____ (1)

(f) The bar chart below shows the mass of phosphate entering the loch each day from different sources in three particular years.

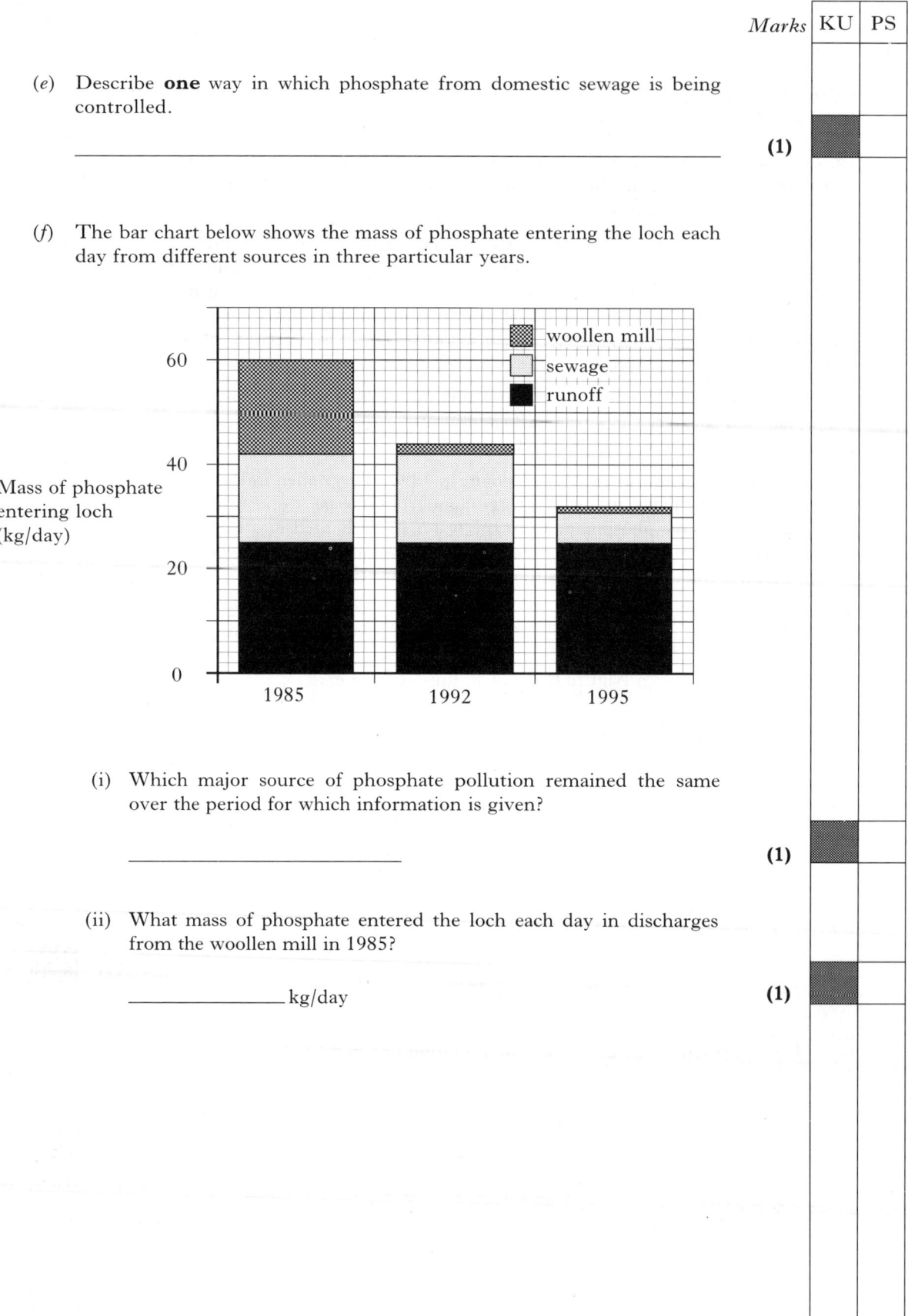

(i) Which major source of phosphate pollution remained the same over the period for which information is given?

_____ (1)

(ii) What mass of phosphate entered the loch each day in discharges from the woollen mill in 1985?

_____ kg/day (1)

14. The map below gives information about acid rain in Europe.

Key
- ■ imported acid rain
- □ home produced acid rain

1 Finland 5 United Kingdom
2 Norway   6 Netherlands
3 Sweden   7 France
4 Denmark

(a) Name the country where 50% of the acid rain is "home produced".

_____ (1)

(b) At point **A**, in the North Sea, the wind normally blows towards the north-east. What information from the map would support this statement?

_____

_____ (1)

(c) The Netherlands (Country 6 on the map) has acid rain, 75% of which is imported.

Complete the pie chart to show the proportions of imported and home produced acid rain in that country.

■ imported acid rain

☐ home produced acid rain

(2)

(d) Acid rain is caused by various gases which pollute the atmosphere. State **one** major source of such gases.

_____

(1)

15. (a) (i) Identify the micro-organism used in the manufacture of each of the following products. Draw a line from each product to the correct micro-organism.

Products	Micro-organism
Beer	
	Yeast
Cheese	
Yoghurt	
	Bacteria
Wine	

(2)

(ii) Choose a word from the list which matches each of the following descriptions and write it into the correct box.

List

Antibiotics
Enzymes
Lactic acid
Insulin

Description	Word
Made by genetically engineered bacteria and used in biological detergents	
Used to prevent the growth of micro-organisms	
Made by bacteria and used to treat diabetes	

(3)

(b) The diagram below shows one method of treating sewage.

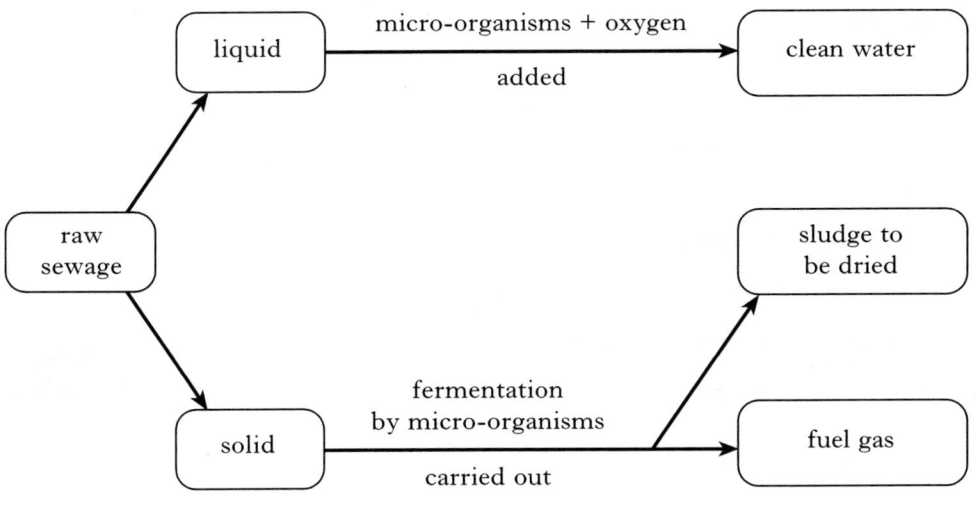

(i) Give the name of the fuel gas produced by fermentation of the solid material.

_____

(1)

(ii) Give **one** advantage of using fuels obtained by fermentation, rather than fossil fuels such as coal and oil.

_____

(1)

(c) The graph below shows the change in the number of micro-organisms in a population.

Complete the table by entering a letter from the graph which matches each of the statements.

Description	Area
Population is increasing most rapidly	
Birth rate and death rate are equal	

(2)

16. The diagram below shows the apparatus used in an investigation of the fermentation of glucose by yeast.

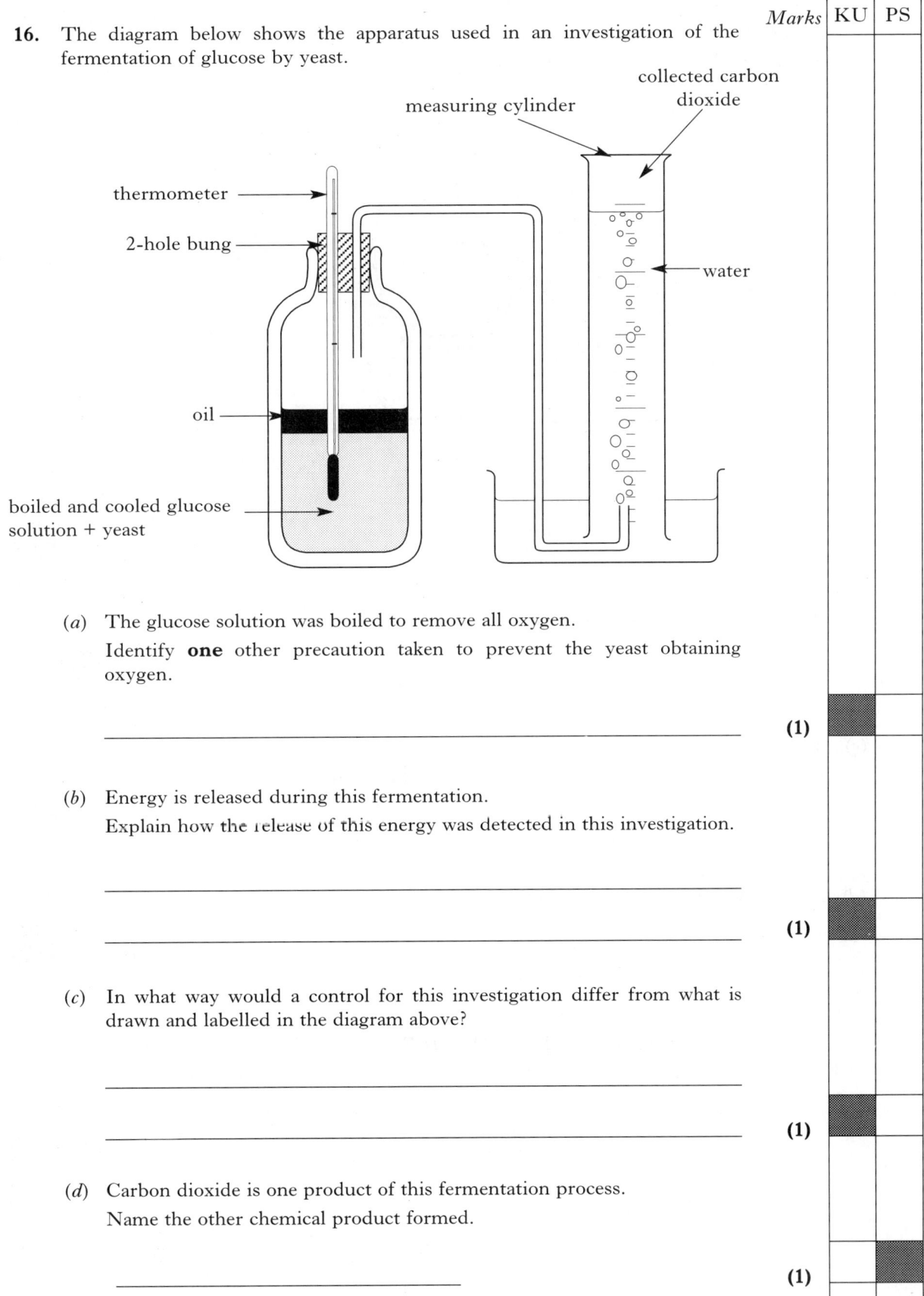

(a) The glucose solution was boiled to remove all oxygen.

Identify **one** other precaution taken to prevent the yeast obtaining oxygen.

_____ (1)

(b) Energy is released during this fermentation.

Explain how the release of this energy was detected in this investigation.

_____

_____ (1)

(c) In what way would a control for this investigation differ from what is drawn and labelled in the diagram above?

_____

_____ (1)

(d) Carbon dioxide is one product of this fermentation process.

Name the other chemical product formed.

_____ (1)

17. The diagram below shows an elbow joint in a person with arthritis. The cartilage in this joint is damaged.

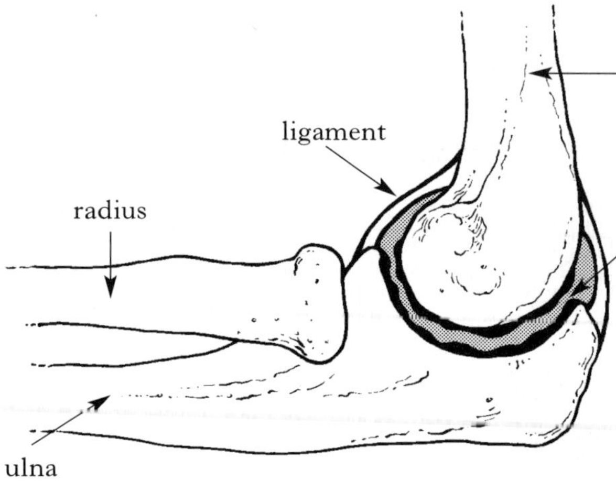

(a) State the function of cartilage in a healthy joint.

_____ (1)

(b) Predict the effect of damaged cartilage on the movement of the joint.

_____ (1)

(c) The elbow joint is an example of a hinge joint.
Describe the range of movement allowed by a hinge joint.

_____ (1)

(d) Name **one** main component of bone.

_____ (1)

[END OF QUESTION PAPER]

SCOTTISH CERTIFICATE OF EDUCATION 1998

MONDAY, 11 MAY
9.00 AM – 10.30 AM

BIOLOGY
STANDARD GRADE
General Level

Marks | KU | PS

1. The following diagram shows part of a food web in Californian scrubland.

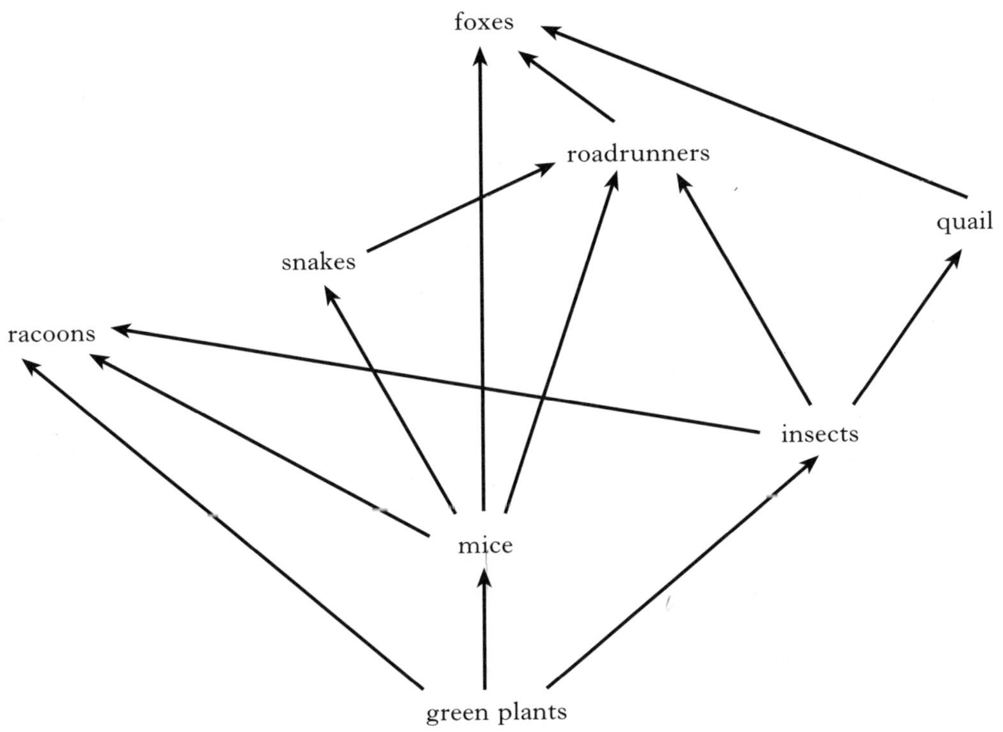

[Food web diagram showing: green plants → mice, insects; mice → snakes, roadrunners, racoons, foxes; insects → roadrunners, quail, racoons; snakes → roadrunners; roadrunners → foxes; quail → foxes]

(a) (i) Which organisms are the producers in this food web?

_____green plants_____ (1)

(ii) Name the process by which producers make food.

_____photosynthisis_____ (1)

(b) (i) Name **two** animals in the food web that are **not** eaten by other animals in this food web.

_____snakes_____ and _____racoons_____ (1)

(ii) Omnivores eat both plants and animals.
Name the omnivore in the food web.

_____ (1)

(c) (i) Using information from the food web, complete the food chain below.

green plants → mice → snakes → roadrunners → foxes (1)

(ii) How many individual food chains in the food web include roadrunners?

_____ (1)

(d) Mice obtain energy from the food they eat. Some of this energy is used for growth.

State **two** other ways in which the mice use this energy.

1 _____

2 _____ (2)

(e) Competition occurs when different organisms have a need for the same food source.

Describe **one** example of competition between two organisms in the food web.

Food source competed for _____ (1)

Competing organisms _____ and _____ (1)

2. The diagram represents a human skeleton.

(a) Name the parts of the body which are protected by the labelled parts of the skeleton.

X protects the __brain__

Y protects the __heart__ and the __lungs__

Z protects the __spine__   (3)

(b) The skeleton protects parts of the body.
State **two** other functions of the skeleton.

1 _____

2 _____   (2)

(c) Which structures hold the bones together at a joint?

__tendons__   (1)

(d) A bone is soaked in dilute acid for several days. It becomes flexible because it still contains elastic fibres.
What part of the bone has been removed by the acid?

__cells__   (1)

3. (a) The grid below refers to structures of plant and animal cells.

A cell membrane	B nucleus	C chloroplast
D cell wall	E cytoplasm	F large vacuole

Use letters from the grid to answer the following questions.
Each letter may be used **once, more than once** or **not at all**.

(i) Which **three** structures are found **only** in plant cells?

cell wall _chloroplast_ _large vacuole_ (1)

(ii) Which structure controls cell division?

_____ (1)

(iii) Which structure controls the movement of substances into and out of the cell?

cell membrane (1)

(b) The concentration of some substances inside and outside three cells is shown in the diagrams below.

cell 1: outside high oxygen, inside low oxygen
cell 2: outside low water, inside high water
cell 3: outside low carbon dioxide, inside high carbon dioxide

Use the numbers from the diagrams above to identify the cells in which the following would occur.

(i) Diffusion **into** the cell of the substance shown.

cell 1 (1)

(ii) Osmosis.

cell 2 (1)

4. The bar chart below shows some information on the components of mycoprotein compared with other foods that are traditional sources of animal protein. Mycoprotein is a food produced by a fungus.

Mass of component (g/100 g of food) vs Food (Cheese, Chicken, Sausage, Mycoprotein) — bars for protein (hatched) and fat (black). Cheese: protein ~26, fat ~33. Chicken: protein ~20, fat ~4. Mycoprotein: protein ~12, fat ~3.

(a) Sausage has 9 g of protein and 24 g of fat per 100 g. **Plot this data** on the bar chart above. (2)

(b) (i) Which food has the highest protein content?

  cheese (1)

  (ii) Which food has the lowest fat content?

  mycoprotein (1)

  (iii) Which foods have more fat than protein?

  cheese (1)

(c) The mycoprotein has 12 g of protein and 3 g of fat per 100 g.
  Calculate the protein to fat content in mycoprotein as a simple whole number ratio.
  Space for calculation 12 : 3

  __4__ : __1__
  protein   fat (1)

5. The diagram below shows the newly hatched young of a trout.

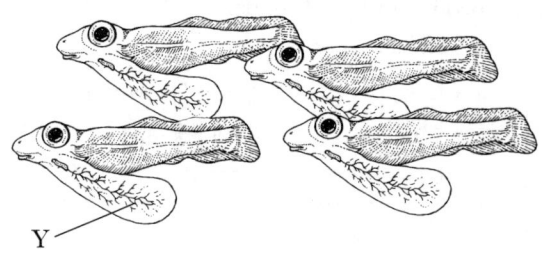

Y

(a) Give the name and function of the structure labelled Y.

Name _____

Function _____ (2)

(b) The following table shows the number of days from egg laying to hatching in trout at different temperatures.

Temperature (°C)	5	10	15	20
Time to hatching (days)	60	40	22	5

(i) Plot a line graph of the data on the grid below.

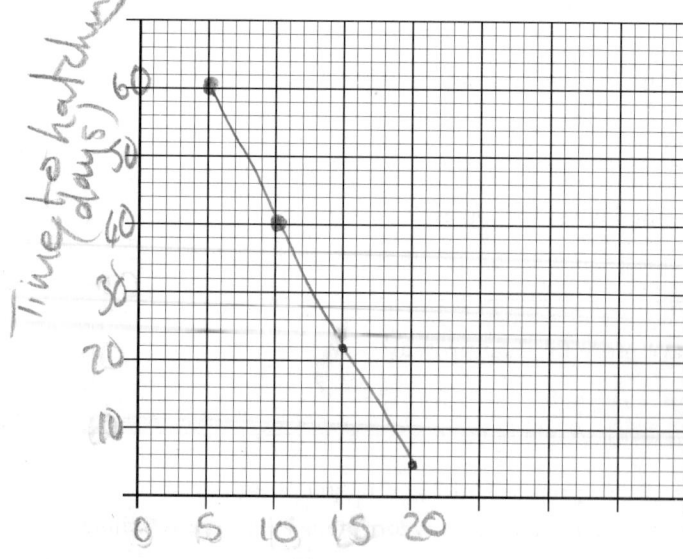

Temperature (°C)

(3)

(ii) What is the effect of increasing the temperature on hatching time?

It speeds up the hatching (1)

6. The family tree below shows the inheritance of comb shape in fowl.

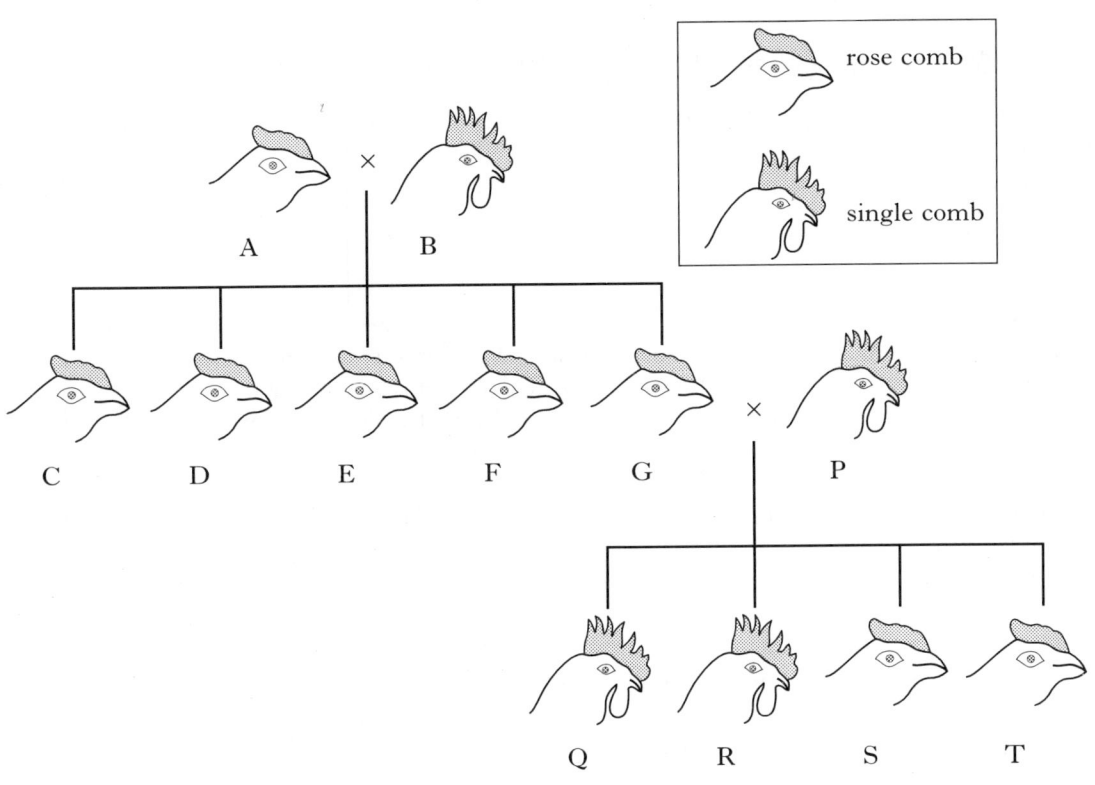

(a) What evidence from the family tree suggests that the gene for single comb is recessive?

_____

_____ (1)

(b) Fowl A is true-breeding.
Identify **all** the other true-breeding fowl in the family tree.

_____ (1)

(c) How many individuals are there in the F$_2$ generation of this family tree?

_____ (1)

7. An investigation was carried out to find the effect of a chemical on the activity of the enzyme amylase. Amylase acts on starch to produce the sugar maltose.

Three test-tubes, A, B and C, were set up with contents as shown below.

A	B	C
6 cm³ starch suspension 4 cm³ water	6 cm³ starch suspension 2 cm³ amylase solution 2 cm³ water	6 cm³ starch suspension 2 cm³ amylase solution 2 cm³ chemical solution

The test-tubes were placed in a water bath at 37 °C.

After 20 minutes, iodine solution was added to each tube to test for the presence of starch.

The results are shown in the table below.

Tube	Starch concentration
A	High
B	Zero
C	Low

(a) Suggest **one** factor about the starch suspension, not shown in the diagrams, which should be the same in each of the tubes at the start.

_____ (1)

(b) Tube A is a control. Explain the purpose of the control.

_____

_____ (1)

(c) Describe the effect of the chemical on the activity of amylase in tube C.

_____

_____ (1)

8. (a) The diagram below shows some of the structures of the human breathing system.

Three of the structures have been arrowed.

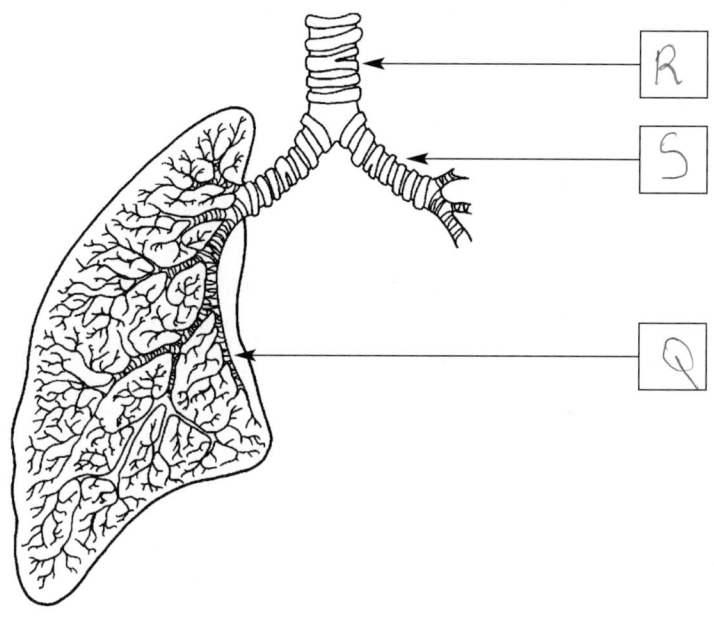

Match the correct letters from the list below to the structures on the diagram by writing the letters in the boxes.

Q — bronchiole
R — windpipe
S — bronchus

(2)

(b) The table below shows the changes in breathing of a person at rest and during exercise.

	Breaths per minute	Volume of air inhaled in each breath (cm^3 per breath)	Volume of air inhaled in one minute (cm^3)
At rest	16	500	8000
During exercise	21	1000	21 000

Describe **two** effects of exercise on breathing.

1 _____

_____

2 _____

_____ (2)

(c) (i) 8000 cm³ of air is inhaled in one minute at rest. 4% of the air we inhale is absorbed into the blood as oxygen.

Calculate the volume of oxygen entering the blood during one minute when at rest.

Space for calculation

Volume _____ cm³ (1)

(ii) The following charts show the relative proportions of 3 gases in two different samples of air.

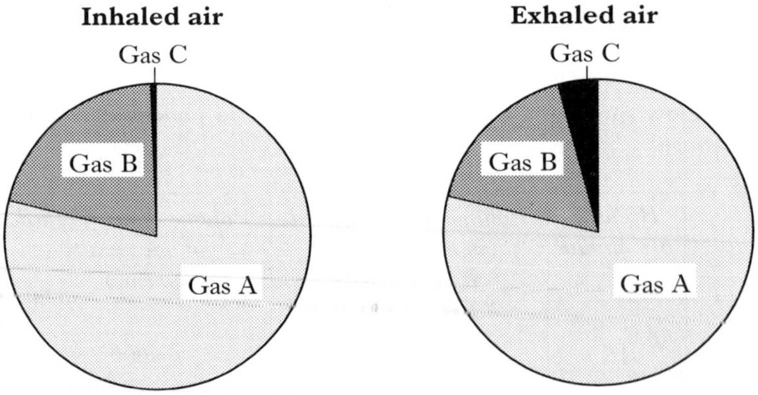

Inhaled air　　　　　　　　**Exhaled air**

Gas C　　　　　　　　　　　　Gas C
Gas B　　　　　　　　　　　　Gas B
Gas A　　　　　　　　　　　　Gas A

Name gas C.

_____ (1)

9. (a) The table below shows the mass of some pollutants entering the air in Britain in one year.

Pollutant	Mass (units)
Carbon monoxide	100
Sulphur dioxide	34
Hydrocarbons	23
Dust	23
Nitrogen oxides	20
Total	200

(i) Use the information from the table to add one line to the pie chart below so that it represents the data correctly. **(1)**

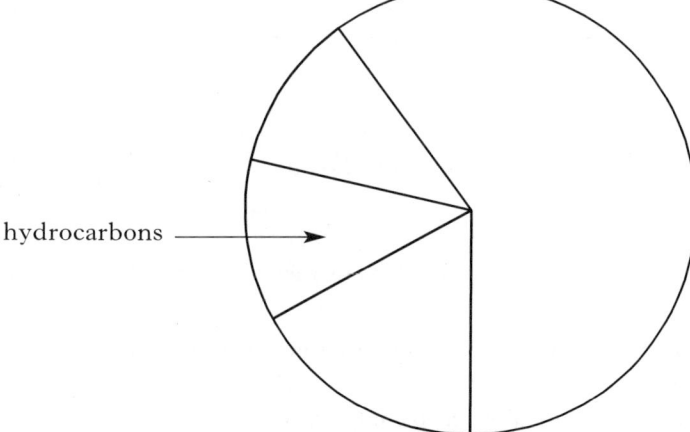

(ii) Label the pie chart to show the correct position of each pollutant. **(1)**

(iii) Calculate the percentage of sulphur dioxide in the total mass of pollutants.

Space for calculation

sulphur dioxide _____ % **(1)**

(b) In 1970, smoke concentrations in the air in Britain were 55 units/m³.
In 1958, they were 165 units/m³.
How many times greater were smoke concentrations in 1958 than in 1970?

Space for calculation

Number of times _____ (1)

(c) Complete the table below by
  (i) naming the missing main source of pollution;
  (ii) giving **one** example of a pollutant from each of the other main sources.

Main source of pollution	Example of pollutant
Domestic	
Agricultural	
	sulphur dioxide

(3)

(d) The list below contains statements about the management of natural resources.

  X Modern agriculture often involves the creation of large areas used to grow one type of crop.
  Y Tropical rain forests are burnt to allow crops to be grown.
  Z Rivers and seas are often used for the disposal of sewage material.

Choose **one** of the statements and describe a problem which may result from it.

Statement _____

Problem _____

_____

(1)

10. (a) The bar chart below shows the ways in which a horse **gains** water over a day.

Volume of water gained per day (litres) vs Method of gaining water: Drinking ≈ 6.5, X = 3.0, Chemical reactions ≈ 2.8

(i) Identify X on the bar chart.

_____ (1)

(ii) Calculate the total daily water gain of the horse.
Space for calculation

_____ litres (1)

(b) The table shows the average daily **losses** of water for the same horse. Complete the table by writing in the missing methods of water loss.

Method of losing water	Volume of water lost per day (litres)
	7·8
Sweat	2·8
	1·2
Faeces	0·5

(2)

11. (a) The grid below contains words and phrases connected with ecology.

A populations	B habitats	C plants
D animals	E abiotic factors	F biosphere

Use letters from the grid to answer the following questions.
A letter may be used **once**, **more than once**, or **not at all**.

(i) Which **two** make up a community?

_____ and _____ (1)

(ii) Which **three** make up an ecosystem?

_____ , _____ and _____ (1)

(b) The following list contains examples of groups of organisms that can be easily sampled.

Group 1: small invertebrates in the leaf litter below trees
Group 2: small invertebrates in the gravel of a river bed
Group 3: species of plants growing in a lawn
Group 4: small invertebrates in the foliage of a small tree
Group 5: small invertebrates on the seashore

Choose **one** of the examples from the list and answer the questions that follow.

Chosen Group Number _____

(i) Name **or** describe a technique which could be used to obtain the sample.

_____

_____

_____ (1)

(ii) Name **two** abiotic factors which might affect the distribution of the organisms in the chosen example.

1 _____

2 _____ (1)

12. Read the passage below and answer the questions which follow.

Pollination of primrose flowers by bees

A species of primrose has two different kinds of flower. They differ from each other in the positions of the stamens and the stigmas in the flowers.

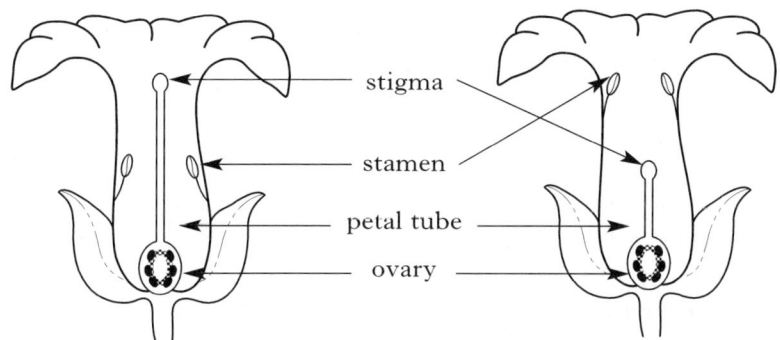

Pin-eyed flower   Thrum-eyed flower

Nectar is produced near the base of the ovary. A bee must push its proboscis (feeding tube) deep into the flower to be able to drink the nectar. In a pin-eyed flower, pollen will stick to the middle of the proboscis. In a thrum-eyed flower, the pollen will stick to the base of the proboscis.

When a bee visits both types of flowers, pollen from one type will be in a position on the proboscis to be brushed on to the stigma of the other type.

(a) Describe the positions of the stamens and stigmas in **both** kinds of primrose flower.

_____

_____

_____ (2)

(b) (i) Primroses attract bees by producing nectar.
Name the structure which produces nectar.

_____ (1)

(ii) What is the name given to the feeding tube of a bee?

_____ (1)

(iii) How does the site of nectar production ensure that a bee will pick up pollen when it drinks the nectar?

_____ (1)

(c) (i) Name the part of the flower in which the female sex cells are produced.

_____ (1)

(ii) What is the name of the stage in the reproduction of primroses in which male and female nuclei join together?

_____ (1)

(d) The table below contains information about five different varieties of apple tree found in an orchard.

Variety of apple tree	Flowering time	Picking time	Ready to eat
Discovery	mid-season	August	August–September
Sunset	mid-season	September	October–December
Merton Beauty	late season	September	September–October
Irish Peach	early season	August	August–September
Idared	early season	October	November–April

Use information from the table to answer the following questions.

(i) The fruit of which variety takes the longest to develop?

_____ (1)

(ii) Which **two** varieties of apple are ready to be eaten in August?

_____ and _____ (1)

(iii) Apple trees need to be cross pollinated with pollen from a different variety of apple tree, in order to produce fruit.

Which variety of tree in the orchard is likely to produce a poor crop of apples?

Use the information in the table to give a reason for your answer.

Variety _____ (1)

Reason _____ (1)

13. (*a*) The diagrams show the skulls of two mammals with the teeth removed.

Carnivore   Herbivore

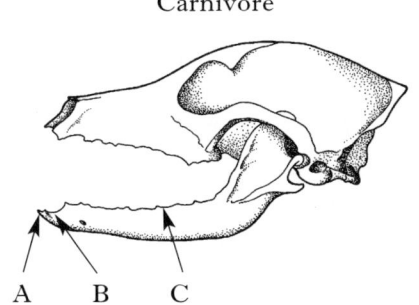 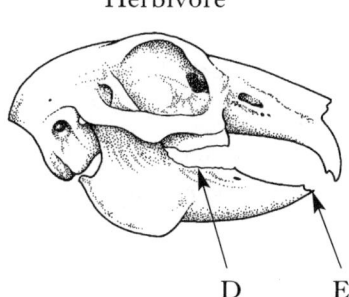

A   B   C   D   E

Complete the table below by
(i) selecting a letter from the diagrams above to indicate the position of each type of tooth;

(ii) selecting a function from the list below.

Piercing and holding
Crushing and grinding
Slicing and tearing

Tooth	Position	Function

(3)

(b) The diagram represents the digestive system of a rabbit.

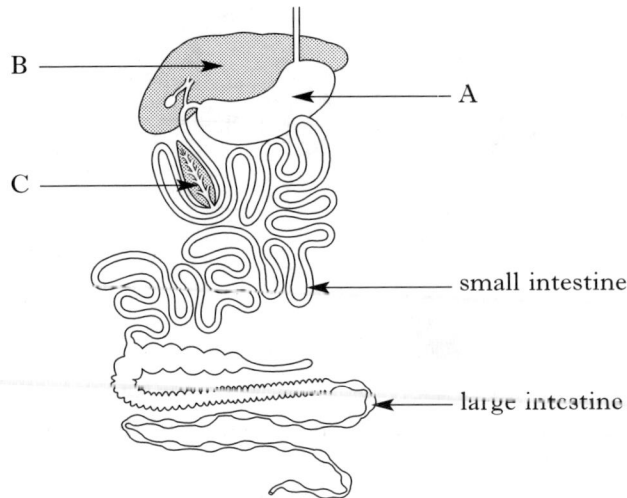

(i) Name the parts labelled with the following letters.

A _____

B _____

C _____ (2)

(ii) What feature of the small intestine, **shown on the diagram**, helps it to carry out its function efficiently?

_____ (1)

(iii) The mass of material which enters the large intestine after digestion is far greater than the mass of faeces eliminated.

Name the substance which is removed from the material as it passes along the large intestine.

_____ (1)

14. The diagram shows an investigation carried out by four pupils into hearing. Each pupil sat in a room with loudspeakers placed all around.

A beep was played from each of the loudspeakers in a random order. The pupil was asked to point in the direction of the loudspeaker which had made the sound.

A record was made showing if the direction indicated was correct or not for each beep.

Each pupil was tested twice,
(i) with one ear uncovered
(ii) with both ears uncovered.

The results are shown in the table.

	One ear uncovered		Both ears uncovered	
	correct	incorrect	correct	incorrect
Pupil A	6	6	10	2
Pupil B	4	8	7	5
Pupil C	7	5	11	1
Pupil D	5	7	8	4
Totals	22	26	36	12

(a) What conclusion can be drawn about the use of two ears rather than one?

_____ (1)

(b) Suggest **two** variables which would need to be kept constant to make certain that the conclusion was valid.

1 _____

2 _____ (2)

(c) Calculate the ratio of correct to incorrect directions for Pupil A with both ears **uncovered**.

Space for calculation

_____ : _____
 correct   incorrect (1)

(d) The total number of beeps made when the pupils had both ears **uncovered** was 48.

Calculate the percentage of beeps for which the correct direction was indicated.

Space for calculation

_____ % (1)

(e) Explain why four pupils were tested rather than just one.

_____
_____ (1)

15. (*a*) The table below shows information about four varieties of oats.

Feature \ Variety	A	B	C	D
Survival at low temperatures	very good	poor	good	poor
Pest resistance	poor	good	poor	very good
Survival in dry conditions	very good	good	poor	very good

(i) Which of the four varieties should a farmer choose for growing in a region with:

1 low temperatures? _____ **(1)**

2 low rainfall and a high number of pests? _____ **(1)**

(ii) Name the procedure of crossing different plant varieties to produce improved characteristics in the next generation.

_____ **(1)**

(iii) Which plant variety should be crossed with variety B to try to produce plants which survive low rainfall and low temperature?

Variety _____ **(1)**

(b) The table below gives some information on plants that have been genetically altered to show new characteristics.

Plant	Examples of new characteristics		
	Resistance to insects	Tolerance to herbicide	Resistance to fungi
cotton	✓	✓	
maize	✓	✓	
oil seed rape	✓	✓	✓
peanut	✓		
soya bean		✓	
tobacco	✓	✓	✓
tomato	✓	✓	

(i) Identify the characteristics which have been given to maize by genetic alteration.

_____

_____ (1)

(ii) Which plants have been given resistance to fungi?

_____ (1)

(c) Bacteria that have been genetically altered, can make products for humans.

Give **one** example of a product made by such bacteria.

_____ (1)

16. (a) The yeast used to make beer converts sugar into alcohol.

The graph below shows the changes in the sugar content of beer while it is being manufactured.

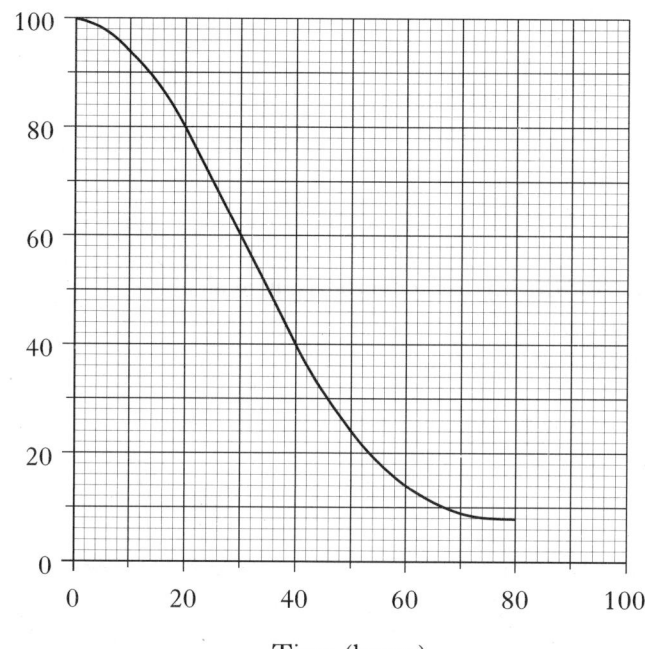

(i) How long does it take for 50% of the sugar to be used?

_____ hours

(ii) During which 10 hour period is there the smallest decrease in the sugar content?

Tick the correct box.

0–10 hours ☐

10–20 hours ☐

60–70 hours ☐

70–80 hours ☐

(iii) What was the sugar content of the beer after 50 hours?

_____ % of original sugar

(iv) The mass of sugar at the start was 500 g.
Calculate the **mass of sugar** remaining after 30 hours.
Space for calculation

Mass of sugar _____ g (1)

(b) (i) Name the process in which yeast converts sugar to alcohol.

_____ (1)

(ii) Name **one** other product of this process.

_____ (1)

(c) Underline the **two** words from the list below which can be used to describe yeast.

single-celled
multi-celled
fungus
bacterium (1)

[*END OF QUESTION PAPER*]